The
Se

WALK ON

The Five Mile Press

The Five Mile Press Pty Ltd
950 Stud Road, Rowville
Victoria 3178
Australia

Email: publishing@fivemile.com.au
Website: www.fivemile.com.au

First published 2005

Designed by SBR Productions, Olinda, Victoria
Edited by Sonya Nikadie
Printed in Australia by Griffin Press

National Library of Australia Cataloguing-in-Publication data
Hodge, Brenda
Walk on: the remarkable true story of the last person sentenced to
death in Australia

ISBN 1 74124 671 7.

1. Hodge, Brenda. 2. Abused women – Western Australia – Biography.
3. Women prisoners – Western Australia – Biography. I. Title.

365.43092

WALK ON

The remarkable true story of the last person sentenced to death in Australia

Brenda Hodge

The Five Mile Press

Contents

APOLOGY TO PETER'S FAMILY AND FRIENDS

Why did I write this book? First, I want to make a public apology to Peter and his family and friends. I am deeply sorry for the hurt I have caused them. Second, writing my story is cathartic. Still battling with old demons, the written form enables me to confront them better than I did in the past. Third, I want to show those who have been used and abused as children that they do not need to feel shame. I want them to learn to love themselves and not hide from the past, just as I am – still – learning to do.

If I can do the last of these things then baring my soul to the world is worth it…

Foreword

I would like to thank Vanish for the wonderful work they do in tracing missing family members. It is through them that I came into contact with Clan (Careleavers of Australia Network).

If I had know about Clan before writing this book I might not have leant so much towards understatement. I might not have worried about those 'carers' and professionals who have called me 'paranoid, neurotic and fanciful' if I had known so many other children had suffered similar traumas to mine. However, I am content to leave my story as it is, and include contact numbers for any readers who might want to rediscover their past.

After being approached by Clan, Senator Andrew Murray (WA) set up the National Senate of Inquiry into Children in Institutions. It was released in August 2004, but submissions will never really close as long as others want to tell their stories. After reading the report, *The Forgotten Australians*, I gained a better understanding of how Victorian children were locked up without committing an offence.

It was also through Vanish that I came into contact with the Forde Foundation, which was set up after completion of the Forde Report, otherwise known as *The Commission of Inquiry into Abuse of Children in Queensland Institutions*, 1999. And it was through the Forde Foundation that I discovered the place I knew as Sandy

Gallop was actually an establishment set up by the government called Karrala House. It was for 'incorrigible girls', a 'quasi-penal institution to facilitate the task of extracting and disciplining "problem girls"' (*Karrala House – Closed Report* 1999). This facility was set up in a vacant female ward of the Ipswich Mental Hospital from 1963 to 1971 in a Brisbane suburb called Sandy Gallop.

Access to this kind of information has cleared up some of the mystery of my life, and has helped me to gain a proper perspective on the past. I'm hoping the following contact details will also help some of the other 500,000 Australians who were 'lost' in institutions last century.

VANISH
199 Cardigan Street, Carlton, Victoria 3053
Tel: (03) 9348 2111
Fax: (03) 9349 4853
Email: vanish@vicnet.net.au

CLAN
P.O Box 164
Georges Hall, New South Wales, 2198
Tel: (02) 9709 4520
Email: support@clan.org.au

FORDE FOUNDATION
43 Peel Street, South Brisbane, Queensland, 4101
Tel: (07) 3224 8862
Freecall: 1800 674 256
Email: forde@merivale.org.au

Prologue

I love the smell of peppercorn trees. I've planted four of them in my backyard, and two of them are now big enough to form a canopy over an old wooden bench where I read the paper and have a cup of tea in the morning, or relax with a glass of wine after work. When the wind is up – as it nearly always is in Geraldton – the leaves make a lovely hushing noise, a familiar sound that has followed me through the quieter times of my life.

It's easy to forget all the violence, neglect and abuse when I'm sitting under my peppercorn trees. It's easy to let go all that pain and anguish, although sometimes the cry of a bird or a little too much wine brings back memories and emotions I had imagined were dormant. Twelve years ago a prison psychologist shocked me by saying, 'Emotions are timeless'. Suddenly I understood a lifetime of depression. I wrote this then.

Turning Point

At the age of 41
I thought I was grown up
but found my emotions
were stunted,

had not developed
past the ages of 4, 6 and 10,
so when she said
'emotions are timeless'
I suddenly understood
my depression. Despair
is the unloved child
fear is the bashed child
anger is the raped child
still within, still fighting
for a voice
at the age of 41 –
a small voice
getting louder

Geraldton Regional Prison, October 1992

I'm not such a 'small voice' any more. I am confident enough to speak my mind about injustices, past and present, because I have been taught by some very special people along the way to love and respect myself despite having done some very unlovable things in my life.

At the age of 33 I killed a man – my de facto – and that is the worst thing one human being can do to another. It's irreversible. There were many times when I said, 'I'm sorry, Peter, please come back!' and for a long time I couldn't forgive myself.

Now, at the age of 53, I sit under my peppercorns, drinking tea, admiring the roses, the frangipanis and the cumquats loaded with early fruit. I watch the insects and the birds. And, in turn, from the back door step, I am watched. Jarrah, the bull-terrier I took in when

he was down on his luck, squints in the sun, looking at me unblinkingly, as if he might be thinking: 'You're at peace. I'm happy. Life's good. Why wasn't it always like this?'

On my way back inside I stoop to scratch the back of his head. It's a long story, Jarrah.

Brenda Hodge, 2005

Walk on, through the wind
Walk on, through the rain
Tho' your dreams be tossed and blown
Walk on…
Walk on…
With hope in your heart,
And you'll never walk alone…'

– From Rodgers & Hammerstein's
'You'll Never Walk Alone'

CHAPTER 1

Fathers and Family

I was a toddler at Uncle George's, in a high chair with a bowl of green peas in front of me. I didn't want them. My mother was angry, stuffing peas into my mouth, Uncle George telling her to 'Leave it, Nan, leave her alone.' My mouth was bulging. I spat the peas out, over my mother, the high chair, the floor.

The next thing I remember is heading down the dark potholed driveway, down Mahoney's Road, flanked by huge old pine trees, and turning out onto the Burwood Highway. I got as far as Nanna Mock's place and then on to the butcher shop next door. I was worn out, so I sat on the step there until they found me.

I knew it was wrong, but running away gave me a powerful feeling of freedom. In the open air and the darkness, where I couldn't be seen, I felt the excitement explorers must feel heading into the unknown. Running away became a theme in my life story. Eventually it led me to Kalgoorlie, to a murder trial, standing in the dock, and the judge asking me if I had anything to say before he pronounced sentence.

Up until the middle of 2003, my only immediate family was my young brother Eddie, and his father, my stepfather, Jack Mock.

Edd and Jack now live in the hills outside Perth. I'm very close to Edd, but I hadn't seen Jack for most of the eleven and a half years years I was in prison or the eight years since. I was angry with him because he'd been in a financial mess and I thought that Edd and I would have to carry the burden when he got sick.

Then, on Tuesday 24 June after almost twenty years, Jack phoned. Edd was in Royal Perth Hospital, he said. He'd had a heart attack. Edd, who'd never drunk or smoked, a sportsman, firefighter, hard worker, Edd, my baby brother, in hospital and, at 49, perhaps not coming out. With the doomsday vision that sometimes comes upon me I saw myself alone in the world, a person without a family.

Then Edd came out of hospital. He had to stop work and Jack stayed with him for a while. Edd's a man with a strong but gentle spirit. Those who know Edd love him, so friends and neighbours in his small community look out for him. A month after he went home, Edd phoned. He asked me if I wanted to talk to a Helen, from an agency called Vanish, in Victoria. He just didn't have the strength. But it was about two women who were looking for us. Sisters.

For three days I thought about this astonishing news – with all its implications – and then I rang Helen. I had two sisters, she told me, Janette, who our mother had when she was 14 years old, born in Melbourne on New Year's Day, 1943, and Carole, who was born two years later. Daniel was born in 1947, and I came along four years later, on 22 February 1951. Edd was born on 10 December 1953. Between the five of us we had five fathers – three of them unknown.

Carole had contacted Vanish. When her parents died she learned that she'd been adopted and she set about tracing her real family. She thought our mother might have died. How did I feel about that,

Helen asked me. 'My mother was a cruel woman,' I said. 'To be honest I'd be quiet relieved to hear that she's dead.'

On 3 August 2003 Carole Baxter rang. 'Hello... Brenda?'

'Carole? How are you?'

We were guarded at first, but when she told me that Nan, as our mother called herself until later in life, had in fact died, I felt immense freedom. I opened up. 'The amazing thing for me, Carole, is that I never knew you existed. How could the old girl have kept it from me?'

'The old girl?'

'That's what Edd and I call her. She called herself Nan. We call her the old girl. But how could she tell me about one baby – she used to tell me about the little baby she had to give away, but that must have been Janette – but not *ever* mention you!'

We swapped notes. I told her that I knew our mother had a child when she was fourteen. The story was that Nan's mother, Marie, died of tuberculosis the year before and her husband, Keith, had remarried – to the housekeeper, possibly. He'd kicked Nan onto the streets. She'd got pregnant, had a baby girl and the baby was taken from her and adopted because she couldn't care for it.

Carole said that in fact our grandfather had kicked both Marie and Nan out of the house. Marie had died in a sanatorium. Whatever the case, someone took a photograph of the baby and my mother carried it with her for as long as I knew her. When she was drunk and almost falling down, she'd show it to me, a fading black and white image of a little girl in a bonnet, and she'd say, 'Ah, well, you are my only daughter!'

The baby, I now know, was Janette, her birth name, Marguerite Dawn. Carole was named Geneva Nanette Caroline.

Nan's five children all grew up in the same area, Melbourne, in the baby boomers era, yet we led such different and separate lives, not knowing that there were five of us. Nan would have liked that. She liked to be mysterious and secretive.

Janette, the eldest, was born at the Royal Women's Hospital in Melbourne on 1 January 1943, and placed in St Joseph's Foundling Hospital, Broadmeadows. Ten months later she was placed in the care of her adoptive parents, a 56-year-old railwayman and his 49-year-old wife. She was brought up in the inner-suburb of Richmond, an only child. Her father died when she was thirteen and Janette lived with her mother until she was married, at 21.

Carole was Nan's second child, born on 11 February 1945, also at the Royal Women's Hospital. Her adoptive parents, like Janette's, were middle-aged, her father a 49-year-old payroll clerk, and her mother, 46. As she said in a letter to me in July 2004, 'My adoption was a "de facto" arrangement. Done by a solicitor. It looks like my mum and dad took me at about three months old. The adoption wasn't finalised until about two years later. I don't know if Nan kept me or I was in a foundling home like Janette.'

Carole grew up in a then working class Melbourne suburb, East Malvern, and like Janette, was an only child. They grew up not far from each other and probably passed each other in the street now and then. Janette told me that she and her mother, when they had some spare money, used to catch the tram to Malvern 'to look in the shops'.

Carole's parents took her to Scotland in 1958, when she was thirteen, to meet her father's family. When they returned she discovered she was old enough to leave school – MacRobertson's Girls' High – so she did. She worked in a bank, then in a computer business.

At the time Carole left for Scotland Janette was sixteen, in her last year of school at Richmond Girls' School. She left school just before turning seventeen, and although trained as a shorthand typist, she preferred to work as a shop assistant until she married at the age of 21, less than four years later. I was eight and going to Doncaster Primary.

Janette had to care for her elderly mother while she was raising a young family of four. Carole, like Edd and me, was childless, but she too had to care for elderly parents – both of whom had a stroke – in her early to mid twenties. Carole says there is documentation in which her parents state their reason for wanting to adopt was so she would care for them in their old age.

Carole and I both had a mature-age education. Carole entered university at 30, studying music and film; I started at 35 (in prison), studying English and Literature. Janette went on to become a very accomplished wife and mother, the centre of a large, loving family. She is the only one out of the five of us who succeeded with normal family relationships.

Nearly sixty years after her birth Carole and I were talking for the first time. We talked for an hour that Sunday morning in 2003, and on the following Tuesday night, after we spoke again, I wrote in my diary: 'Had another long talk with Carole. She's great!' But at the foot of the page: 'Later on, fell into a heap, couldn't stop crying – have to see [my psychologist] on Thursday.'

A fortnight later I resumed a genuinely warm relationship with my stepfather Jack. I was no longer angry with him, but the emotions were starting to swing. Apart from the worry about Edd's health the old volcanic rumblings – the fears I had always lived with – were making me physically ill.

I felt for both my sisters. Each of them had been brought up in Melbourne, ignorant of each other, the only child of an elderly couple.

They were now grieving for the 'real' mother they never knew. Grieving for the mother-daughter bond said to be an intrinsic part of our sense of self. Grieving for a lost childhood without siblings.

They didn't miss out on much. I was the sister who had that 'real' mother, had the siblings, had the family life. It was far from normal. Far from happy.

In my first nine years I had no less than four father figures. I spent my early years believing my father was dead. I was two when Jack Mock married my mother and I loved him, called him Dad and waited anxiously for him to come home from work each day. But my mother put a lot of energy into trying to turn me against him.

'He's not your real father. Your real father is Jimmy White. He was a soldier, but now he's in heaven.'

Sometimes she'd show me a photo of Jimmy White. A large sepia studio study, it showed a man in a trim AIF uniform, stiff slouch hat at a jaunty angle. I spoke to my real father, Jimmy White, all the time. He was in heaven, and I had him mixed up with God, the 'Our father who art in heaven'. In my first year at Wonga Park State school I rushed forward when the children of fallen soldiers were called on to place a wreath at the flagpole. I was so proud of my dad that day. Then I came home from school. Danny, my older brother, must have told my mother what had happened.

'You stupid bitch!' She was screeching. 'He didn't die in the war! He got drunk and walked under a car!'

She had always spoken lovingly of him, implied that he died a hero in the war – my hero – and now she despised him. He was just a useless drunk.

I must have decided to push all this information and pain aside, and I continued to talk to Jimmy White when I was punished and locked in my room or the dunny out back. I talked to Jimmy White when I learned to climb out of windows when everyone else was asleep. Unlike Jack, who spent long hours at work during the day, and at night wasn't allowed in my room, Jimmy White was with me all the time. He was the only friend I had.

Many years later, my sister Carole sent me Jimmy White's death certificate and said his family called him a drunk and 'a bastard of a man'. But I know he was there for me, whenever I needed him, when we lived at Wonga Park. When life was more good than bad.

My third father figure was Uncle John, a good man. Gentle, softly spoken, he was a Chinese chef married to Aunty Thel, who had been a whore and was now a fanatical Roman Catholic. My mother sent me to live with them during one of her great escapes from married life, and I stayed with Uncle John and Aunty Thel from the age of six to eight. They wanted to adopt me, but I wanted, I remember telling them, 'to go home with Jack and the boys.' I remember sensing their discomfort. Children are so selfish.

I found out about a fourth father – my biological father – when I went back home. In a trunk under the house Jack kept his photographs and copies of sporting magazines. I was sifting through the photographs and Danny was cleaning the chain on his bike. He looked over. 'Leave them alone, they're not yours.'

'Why? Dad doesn't mind.'

'Oh yeah – well he's not your father anyway.'

'I know that. My father's dead.'

'No he's not. Your father lives over in Port Melbourne. His name is Harry. And Mum goes to see him, so there!'

I ran inside, blubbering, and she sat there, stony-faced. 'Yes, that's right. Your brother should keep his trap shut. And if you don't shut up I'll give you something to really cry about!'

The sense of rejection – that my father would see my mother, but not want to see me – has stayed with me, to a dwindling extent today, for forty-five years.

I finally met my biological father when I was eight or nine. One night my mother opened my bedroom door, and there was a stranger standing next to her. 'This is your father. He has a wife and another little daughter now. They're going to live in Brisbane.' I couldn't speak, couldn't move. I was numb. The man mumbled, 'Look after yourself' and turned and went. A year later I tried to kill myself.

I was happiest of all, in my early childhood, at Uncle George's orchard in Burwood, about 23 kilometres from the centre of Melbourne. Uncle George was Jack's uncle, my mother was his housekeeper, and she took Danny and me in tow. The Mocks had several orchards all joined together, and I have a clear memory of bouncing on the back of a trailer being pulled by a tractor, hanging on, laughing and loving it, as, loaded with boxes of peaches packed in straw, it slowly drove its way over the bumps to the packing shed. I was happy at Uncle George's, hanging around his black boots and long legs in trousers held up with braces, as he fed the chooks vegetable peelings and stale bread. I love the smell of orchards, at blossom time and picking time. But when I ran away from Uncle George's that night, the night my mother fed me the peas, I began down a path that a happy little tacker could never have dreamed of.

Stored in all our memories are reverberations. Moments that are later echoed so that we recall an episode in our past and recognise it as significant or as a portent of what was to come. Things happened, when I was a toddler, that in my later life were repeated or echoed in a more sinister way.

Paradoxically, my years as a toddler at Uncle George's orchard and then at Wonga Park were probably the most pleasurable of my life. Jack married Nan when I was two and the next year we moved to Wonga Park. It was a simple weatherboard house with a dunny out the back but it was lovely. You could sit on the back steps in the early morning and see the Dandenong Mountains, blue hills layered with blankets of fog. Magpies chortled, kookaburras laughed. Whipbirds cracked their whip and the grass was icy under my bare feet as I scampered out to find a place to pee.

The dunny terrified me. I was a tot and had an understandable terror of falling into the hole under the seat, into the stench of the unimaginable darkness down there. There were spiders, too, hairy monsters we called Triantiwontigongs, that scuttled across the walls when disturbed, retreating into the darkness where, I just knew, they lay in wait, ready to pounce. Danny would throw spiders in curled leaves at me, for fun, and I still have a fear of them. I stayed out of the thunderbox as often as I could.

But Nan locked me in there anyway. I was so terrified, I would freeze. I knew if I made a fuss she would leave me in there longer. It was my first experience of solitary confinement and it left me feeling weak and sick, as it did ten years on and at various other times in my adult life.

I was a bed-wetter, of course. The harder I tried not to the more I did it. Nan would go into a fury. 'You dirty little bitch! Get these sheets out to the wash-house!'

I was too short to wash them in the laundry tub but I could put in the sheets and soak them. Later, she'd boil them in the copper and grate Velvet soap into the cauldron. Then she'd lift them out on a wooden stick, wring them, rinse them in water stained with Reckitt's Blue, wring them out again and finally hang them to dry on a long line supported by wooden props. It was fascinating to watch, but always from a distance.

On weekdays Jack went to work as a mechanic at Fisherman's Bend, near Port Melbourne. Danny was at school and Edd was still a baby, so Nan left me to myself most of the day. In winter, alone in the front lounge room, I'd spend the time leafing through the *Australian Encyclopaedia*, or diving my plump little hand under the cushions of the green lounge chairs, always hoping that I'd find a halfpenny, a lolly, or some other treasure. Never finding one didn't deter me. It was the search that was the fun.

Other times I sat on the arm of the old maroon-covered couch and pressed my nose against the window, watching my breath condense on the inside of the glass while raindrops glittered and trickled down the outside. It wasn't warm in the house until the fire was lit in the evening, but it felt cosy to be inside watching the gum trees and native bushes being blown this way and that by the wild, wet weather. I longed for that feeling again, of being inside looking out, when I was homeless and on the streets in my teenage years.

In the spring and summer I spent all my days outside. Sometimes I tagged along with Danny and the boy next door, but I had trouble keeping up with them and once we were out of sight of the house they would bolt off into the bush, leaving me to find my own way home. I never got lost and I never felt frightened. The bush was my first home. There I spent hours building fairy dens with moss or lying on my back in the natural, leafy mulch watching dragonflies hover and whiz away. If I was near pine trees, used as windbreaks around orchards, I would make a bed out of pine needles and lie in it listening to the wind hushing through the branches.

Late in the afternoon on weekdays I'd sit on the grassed embankment out the front of the house and wait to see Jack in the distance, riding his bike home from Croydon station. On pay day, in his haversack, he'd have Allen's Steamrollers or Kool Mints and he'd produce them while Nan called out, 'Stop spoiling them! You'll ruin their appetite!'

She needn't have worried. There never was enough food, as I remember. Usually 'tea' was rabbit stew and vegies from the garden. In the afternoon the rabbits came up onto the back lawn and into the vegetables, so she'd go out with a shotgun. She'd kill a couple, chop their heads off on the chopping block, then skin and cook them straight away. This meant the meat was usually tough and dry and it was always peppered with gunshot and small bones. One night as we were spitting them out and picking through the stew Danny declared he'd had enough. Nan just glared at him and went on feeding Edd in his high chair.

Edd mimicked Danny: 'I don't want mine.' Nan picked up the bowl, half full of stew and mashed potatoes, and emptied it on her baby's head.

Danny could do no wrong in Nan's eyes.

When I was four my mother often put me in the care of a teenage boy who lived nearby. I'm not sure why she did this. I assume she must have paid him a small amount. Naturally enough, I looked up to him.

'You do as Eric (not his real name) tells you,' she'd say to me, delegating her responsibility onto him. He had one other task, besides looking after me. Each day he would chop the wood and stack it in rounds away from the house. One afternoon as I watched him chop, and collect chips to start the fire in the old Metters stove, he sat down on the grass and told me to sit with him. Then he told me to lie down and pulled off my pants. I wanted to get up and go but he was quickly on top of me, pushing down on my chest and telling me to keep quiet. Nan called out. 'Come on you two! What are you up to?'

Could she see us? She was uphill and should have been able to. I started having some sort of anxiety attack and would have cried out, but Eric put his hand over my mouth, going 'Ssh-ssh!'

I can't recall what happened after that. I don't know what he did. I can only recall being terrified that I would be in trouble with my mother.

Eric continued to be a constant visitor to our house and molested and screwed me off and on for the next nine years (in between girlfriends, generally) until I left home aged 14. I'm sure my mother knew what he was up to, but she never asked me about it or tried to put a stop to it. Looking back I suspect it suited her purpose to have me 'experienced'.

CHAPTER 2

A Mother

In 1956, a few weeks before I turned five, I started school. Wonga Park primary was a one-room, one teacher school. Learning to swim was part of the curriculum for schools in the '50s and we had our swimming lessons in a dam at the back of the old pine plantation. We'd all march down, clutching our togs and towels, watching out for snakes as we went. The dam water was muddy, more so when it was stirred by a dozen or so kids, but on a hot summer day any water was good. I loved it. I loved going blackberrying, too. Blackberry bushes grow as big as houses in Victoria and Danny would throw a plank or an old sheet of corrugated iron into the bush and pick berries from it while I picked from the sides. Nan made it into jam, and we'd eat it all year round for lunch, spread on scones.

One day I wandered in from the blackberrying to see a car at the front door and people buzzing about. The lady across the road swept up and grabbed me. 'You're staying at our place tonight, Dorothy, your mummy's going to hospital, but don't worry, she'll be alright. Come on, and I'll run you a nice, warm bath.'

They had a big brick house with a new white bath and a hot water tap. We had an old enamel bath with just a cold water tap. We had to pour hot water from the kettle. It was bliss, floating in warm water in the neighbours' lovely new bath, but at the same time I was upset about my mother's dramatic disappearance. In the luxury of the bath and my nervous apprehension for my mother I lost control of my bladder. I was deeply ashamed. Once again I had shown myself to be a dirty little bitch.

(It took me almost half a century to find out what happened to Nan that day. Jack told me recently. She had delivered a stillborn child, a daughter. He can hardly bring himself to talk about it to this day.)

Then Auntie Thel and Uncle John came into my life. I'd never heard of them, but suddenly there they were, two people pulling up outside the house in a Holden EJ. We went out a few times with them, mostly to the beach and one night to the drive-in to see *Annie Get Your Gun*. Then without a word of explanation or goodbye from Nan, I was packed into the yellow car with a few clothes and taken to their home in Fawkner, on the edge of the city. It was an old brick house with rendered walls and red roof tiles, a small, well-established garden, and Old World roses at the entrance.

I was shown my room – a small room at the back of the house that had once been Dorothy's, Auntie Thel's oldest daughter. Dorothy, a young woman of about nineteen, had moved into a blue bungalow out back with banana passionfruit vines creeping along one wall and a little sign on the door saying Shangri-La. She lived there with her boyfriend.

'This is your new home, dear,' Auntie Thel said, putting my clothes away, 'and we've got to give you a new name. We've already got a Dorothy, and we can't have two! What about your second name?'

'Brenda?' 'Yes, we'll call you Brenda, there's a good girl.'

Then she gave me a broom and told me to sweep the pavers outside the kitchen. I must have been sweeping furiously, in a rage, because the handle snapped and at the same time so did I. I bolted. I ran out the front, down the street, up another street, around the corner, and on and on.

All the streets looked the same. No trees to speak of, just houses and cement footpaths, and when I realised I was lost I slowed down and walked. I was just starting to enjoy myself when a woman – a friend Thel had phoned – stepped out from nowhere and said, 'Hello Brenda, your Auntie Thel is looking for you.' She took me back along the streets until Dorothy met us halfway, handcuffed my child's hand with her long red fingernails and marched me the rest of the way back in silence.

When Uncle John came home we had spaghetti bolognaise – the first of hundreds I was to have at Fawkner. Uncle John was a Chinese chef and he hated spaghetti bolognaise, but that was the only meal Auntie Thel could cook. Why he let her cook I'll never know. Apart from the occasional fish and chips from the shop we always had banana sandwiches for lunch and spaghetti bolognaise for dinner.

Gradually I settled in at Aunty Thel's. School was close by and there were swings and slides on the way. I lost the feeling of always being hungry and I was never belted or threatened. And there was the television. Back home at Wonga Park we didn't have one; the wireless was our entertainment. *The Air Adventures of... Biggles! Tarzan*, *Blue Hills* and *Dad 'n' Dave*. But at Faulkner a friend of Auntie Thel's, three blocks away, had an Astor 17-inch, and every Saturday night we had an early spaghetti bolognaise, changed – me into pyjamas and brunch coat – and walked around to the friend's place.

I'd never seen TV before. Now I could see manly Lloyd Bridges fighting aquatic evildoers in *Sea Hunt*, and, best of all, cool Cookie, compulsively combing his hair in *77 Sunset Strip*, a street apparently peopled exclusively by rich and gorgeous Americans driving shiny red and white convertibles.

In summer we went swimming at a park near Pentridge Prison, 'the Bluestone Lodge'. We'd paddle in a cement pool and sit on a rug under shady trees.

About ten years later, on 3 February 1967, Ronald Ryan was hanged in Pentridge, the last person in Australia to be executed by law. The little girl paddling in the pool outside the prison's bluestone walls would grow up to become the last person in Australia to be sentenced to death in a court of law.

The sentence was commuted, but it was still a kind of death for me.

Walking home from school one afternoon I saw Nan walking towards me.

'How are you?'

'Good. I don't wet the bed much now.'

'That's good. You should put some powder on to stop the smell and the rash.'

That's all I can remember of the conversation. She walked part of the way with me and then turned towards the railway station, stopping for a moment to straighten the seams in her stockings.

Auntie Thel and Uncle John had been kind, and I'll always be grateful to them for happy memories, but I missed Jack and Edd. No matter what, I wanted to go 'home'.

After my second summer at Fawkner Nan returned home and sent for me.

I was about eight when I went back to 29 Tram Road, Doncaster. It was stinking hot. Jack, Nan, Thel and Uncle John were sitting in the backyard having drinks. I was wearing shorts and a little cotton top, climbing up and down the wooden slats on the foundation at the house – showing off. I was happy.

Doncaster was still largely paddocks and orchards. The road at the front of our house was no more than an orchard track rutted where a tractor had sunk into the mud. Alongside and built up higher was Tram Road, used by the Heidelberg painters half a century before when they travelled to the countryside from Box Hill. Draught horses clopped along early in the mornings as the milkman delivered bottles and took away the empties left out on the porch. Children travelled along it in buses, going to and from school.

We used to walk to school. Doncaster was where Danny was a schoolyard bully; I was always in trouble for asking too many questions in class and Edd got bounced on his head by a teacher one day – I don't know why. The teacher grabbed him by the legs, held him upside down and drove his head into the ground. When the old girl heard about it she went up in a rage to see the headmaster, but she didn't get anywhere because she was drunk.

My school reports – I've still got them – show I was good at the work when I applied myself, but spent too much time daydreaming. When I had a seat near a window I would watch birds, trees, clouds – anything that sent me off into a trance. I paid a bit more attention to arithmetic, because we 'got the cuts' – strapped on the palm of the hand – if we couldn't stand up and recite times tables (multiplication) – and you were rapped smartly on the knuckles with a ruler if, like me, you were caught writing with the left hand.

Because Jack was always working and Nan was either drunk or off into the city, or both, we never had any help with homework. The old encyclopaedias helped me out with subjects like history and nature study, but not with arithmetic or algebra. I spent a lot of time doing projects that required illustrating, neglected everything else, and spend the rest of my study time doing detailed pencil drawings of birds, cats, dogs and horses. I also copied, in great detail, women's faces from images in magazines and newspapers.

After school, if Nan had already gone to work, there was always a scramble to see if there were any bickies in the canister: Arnott's Teddy Bears, Anzacs. Sometimes we were lucky, or sometimes there was some bread left and we made up slabs of bread and jam. I'm not sure whether my memory of food shortages is exaggerated or not, but I do remember Jack telling Nan that she was spending too much money on grog and not enough on food. At primary school I sometimes put my hand up to go to the toilet just before the lunch bell. Then I'd systematically go through the schoolbags hanging in the passageway, taking an apple here, a Vegemite or a peanut butter sandwich there. My meal chosen, I'd go to the toilets and eat sitting on the bowl. It wasn't what the hygiene manuals recommended but eight-year-olds hold different views on what's disgusting, and I must have been a tough kid. I was seldom sick. Once, however, I fell ill with the flu. The old girl was angry. It meant she had to stay home to look after me, cook dinner, do the housework. After two days she snapped: 'That's enough. You can go back to school tomorrow. You're not that sick.'

I walked through wet grassy paddocks the next morning. There was a bitter frost, I was sweating under my jumper and my head was spinning. Halfway up the hill I stopped, looked back at the roof our house and thought to myself: 'I will never get married, and I will never have children. I am only eight years old, but I never want a child to hate me as much as I hate my mother!'

Children are resilient. I was able to forget about these things for long periods of time as I made my own fun in life. I found a busted old saddle in a tip near our house, took it home, tied it to the handrail on our back porch, and spent many hours riding my new horse. I was Zorro, the Lone Ranger (Hi-ho Silver!) or Hoss from *Bonanza*. My steed was white or a black, galloping wildly over the plains, halting in a cloud of dust to rear and neigh on clifftops, or he walked a slow clop clop by the river – my horse could be and could do whatever I wanted. We had a TV by this time, so the American West became my mental escape from all things unpleasant in life and *Bonanza* was the best! – there was no mother in *Bonanza*.

People had a strong work ethic in the '50s, and our family was no exception. Jack worked two jobs for nine years to get us kids through school and pay the mortgage. And Nan, a hard drinker, was also a hard worker. A ballroom dancing teacher in the city, at Mickey Powell's Dance Studio, she kept our house clean and took in ironing, although I often had to do the ironing and cook dinner after school.

Little Girls Are Made of Mother*

*I am nothing nobody a nuisance don't come whingeing
to me with your troubles she says putting on thick
red lipstick lady of the night nylon stockings don't
forget to put out the chops for tea do the ironing
wash the dishes
shut up I say softly and whack cop it
across the face don't won't cry sit stunned
and don't forget to clean the bath tonight*

Greenough Regional Prison, 28 April 1993

*This title is borrowed from a poem by Ania Walwicz

As well as going into rages, she could also be deliberately and slowly cruel. Now and then she would line the three of us up, giving each of us a good hiding with a belt until one of us – usually me – owned up to some misdemeanour. I often took the blame for Danny, I so much wanted to please him. I think I got more floggings than the boys and I grew up believing it was because I was a girl.

Nan took to sleeping on the couch in the lounge room instead of with Jack and sometimes she would smash things up during the night. Her story was that an unknown force had whizzed around the room smashing things. But no matter what sort of night she had, she always got up the next morning, did the washing and went to work. She was very stoic and she was very melodramatic. I suppose this helped her to deal with whatever demons she was fighting.

My mother was tiny – about 160 centimetres in heels – muscular but lithe. A perfectionist, she spent hours practising dancing, even at home on her own. When she went on drinking binges she didn't eat and got thin and haggard.

When she was not going to work she loved wearing slacks and very brief shorts – so brief that the cheeks of her bum showed if she bent forward ever so slightly. She complained about not having big enough breasts and stuffed pads down her bra when she went to work. Before going she would sit in front of her mirror to 'put on her face'. Foundation first, then pencilled eyebrows, blue or green eyeshadow, rouge and, finally, the red lipstick. Then she took her auburn hair out of curlers, teased it up, and sprayed it into a solid mass. But no amount of make-up or smart clothes could cover her inner rage. My mother carried it with her like a stone around her neck.

She was born Beryl Nanette MacKenzie on 7 July 1927, at a nurse's home in Rushall Crescent, North Fitzroy, Melbourne. Nan didn't like her father; she called him 'a rich bastard'. I got the feeling she liked her mother, but can't remember her saying anything in particular about her. We knew our extended family on Jack's side, but not on Nan's. She kept everything to herself, not enabling us to understand why she was the way she was: always angry!

I knew Nan's mother had died of tuberculosis, but I didn't know, until my sister Carole told me in 2003, that because of it she and Nan were kicked out of home by my grandfather. I had thought my grandmother had died at home and her 14-year-old daughter, my mother, was kicked out because she was pregnant with Janette.

She learned to be tough early, as a result. She saw herself as strong, stoic and enigmatic, and she certainly had a pig-headed or strong-willed temperament, something all her children inherited. She was a depressive and I seem to have inherited that from her too.

Nan just didn't like kids. We never had a birthday party at home with friends invited around. Kids would have made a mess in the house; kids would have been noisy; too many kids would have been too hard to control. I remember one of my birthdays: Edd and I sat out on the back lawn, under a willow tree, with a piece of cake and a glass of cordial. It was a butter cake with orange icing, bought from the cake shop. It was a luxury, but I was old enough then – nine or 10 – to know it wasn't a proper birthday cake, and I felt aggrieved. I didn't think it unusual that we'd been sent outside while Nan stayed inside – that was the norm.

Nan had nothing nice to say to me. When I asked her what colour my hair was, she said, 'Mouse brown.' When I asked what colour my eyes were, she said, 'Green, you've got cat's eyes.'

Mostly I can't forgive her for beating me without mercy, for selling me to drunks, for trying to make my young life a replica of her own. Sexually abused children often become promiscuous adults and I believe Nan may have been sexually abused as a child. She should, then, have protected me from the same sort of abuse.

I can feel sympathy for her now. But emotionally I still feel anger. Anger is fear in daytime clothes. But I don't have to fear her anymore: she's dead and gone. It's sad, but I never have and never will love my mother. I am only just learning to love myself.

CHAPTER 3

Horses and Grief

Although I usually 'borrowed' horses, I was ten when I was given permission to take Toby, a chestnut cob kept tethered in the open paddocks around us by his owner, a recently married young woman with a new home and a baby. She was happy to let me ride the horse anytime to give him the exercise. I'd pinch apples from the orchards on the way home from school and take them to him and watch him chomp them down. After the ride I'd fill Toby's water bucket, give him a hug and when the late afternoons got crisp throw a canvas rug over his back.

I was in my first year at Templestowe High and the horse was my anchor. Otherwise I was adrift. My brothers now went to different schools, the few girlfriends I had were older, in their teens, and only interested in boys. At home Jack's jobs meant he was only around for short periods at weekends. Nan was almost always drunk and always angry. I was often late for school, sometimes went home at lunch time when no one was there, and more frequently didn't go to school at all. Instead I'd throw a bridle on Toby, ride him down to the river and spend the day with the sun on my back and a warm breeze in my face. The Warrandyte River was beautiful then, crystal clear, and I'd have a swim and let the water massage my shoulders and feet while I lay against a rocky spillway. Afterwards I'd sink into the long grass on the riverbank listening to the whipbirds cracking and the bell-birds tinkling.

One day I came back from the river on a horse I had 'borrowed', a magnificent piebald stallion, a good ride. We were trotting down the road towards home when Nan appeared on the back verandah. The school must have told her I was wagging and she had come home early to catch me in the act.

'Get off that animal at once!'

I looked at her, dug my heels in, and galloped away with great delight. I would cop a flogging – a bad one – when I got home that night, I knew that, but I was going to get one anyway and I might as well enjoy the rest of the day.

I got my flogging, a ritual my mother enjoyed. Usually it began with Nan sitting at the kitchen table smoking and drinking when I came home from school. 'Go to your room and get your clothes off.' I knew what was going to happen, I had plenty of time to think about it. I would sit in my room naked for up to half an hour, dreading what was to happen.

'This is to teach you a lesson,' she would say when she finally came in. 'I'm doing this for your own good.' Then she would lay into me with a strap – an old army belt with the buckle cut off. I know now why she made me lie on the bed and only hit me on the buttocks or around the torso – it was so the red welts and eventual bruises would not be seen by others. These floggings started pre-primary age at Wonga Park, went on through Doncaster Primary and continued until my early days at Templestowe High School. The bedwetting went right through my high school years, right up until I stopped living with Nan. It seems there was a connection.

This time my flogging, for my 'joyride' on the piebald stallion, only made me more defiant. I decided I was going to run away, ride Toby to Sydney.

I talked about it at school with a girl I could trust and who gave me some smuggled provisions for the 1,000-kilometre journey: Superman and Donald Duck comics, and a big bag of broken Brockhoff's from her mum's corner shop. I was ready to go. Next afternoon Toby and I rode off into the sunset.

To get to Sydney Road I had to ride through Templestowe to Balwyn to Heidelberg – where a tram almost made mincemeat of us – past Pentridge Prison and on to Fawkner. By now it was dark and cold and I decided I should call in and say goodbye to Aunty Thel.

'Why don't you have some dinner here, dear,' Thel said, 'sleep the night in a warm bed and then in the morning you'll be right as rain to go to Sydney. Tie up your horse to the clothesline. C'mon.' It sounded good, and after a feed and a hot bath I fell asleep, cosy under the blankets in the spare room bed. Then I was awake. My mother was dragging me out of bed by the hair, drunk and screeching. 'Do you know how much you've cost me for taxi fares! Get dressed! You're going home. I might ring the police and have you hung for horse theft!'

Then she went silent. A bad sign. But I wasn't scared. I knew I could endure whatever she dished out. And I knew my chance to escape would come again. One day, I told myself, I'll be free of you.

Later in the same year, I took an overdose of Bex powders and whatever else was in the bathroom cabinet. Nan made several suicide attempts through the years, so I imagine this was another copycat 'coping strategy'. I can't remember what happened after I took the medicines, but I didn't go for a stomach pump, so it can't have been too bad.

Nan's reaction to this was to send me to see her psychologist; once a week I had to catch a bus into city central. Jack's reaction was to buy me a pony from the pound. It was the best thing anyone had ever done for me.

Chiquita was a bay mare, about thirteen hands high, with a beautiful temperament. I don't know how she ended up in the pound, but a friend of Jack's told him about her, said we could have her for £20 – a lot of money for Jack to find – and his friend drove us to Heidelberg where they legged me up and sent me off down the road.

My own horse! I was free! I was in heaven. Chiquita and I set off for home. Between Heidelberg and Templestowe a large, long bridge spans a river. I had ridden nearly halfway over the bridge when Chiquita was hit by a truck, sent spinning on her side, sliding along the bitumen. I saw her lying there as the truck driver was shaking me. 'Are you alright? Where do you live?'

I was in shock, but eventually told him where I lived. It was on his way; he would let my parents know. I caught Chiquita and slowly and painfully we starting walking home. I was getting close to Templestowe High when I saw Jack running towards us. He must have run five kilometres and when he reached us I started crying.

'What's wrong? Are you hurt?'

'No,' I blubbered. 'I've pissed my pants; what's the old girl going to say?'

When we got home it was getting dark. Nan was not impressed about me having a horse, but didn't say too much. We made a temporary corral at the back of the house near my bedroom and Chiquita stayed there at night.

During the day, I tethered her out in nearby paddocks. The lush grass and wild oats made her fat and shiny and later, when the grass dried, I put her out in the SEC paddock, a 15-hectare paddock with a creek running through it, trees for shade, and fences to stop a quick pony from straying. Riding-school horses in the paddock kept her company.

I made friends with a girl my age who lived on the other side of the paddock, literally, and on the other side of the tracks metaphorically. She had a grey pony club horse, a shiny new saddle with lambswool under it, and a polished riding crop. We got along fine, and spent most weekends riding together, swimming in the river and chasing boys. Meanwhile I was wagging school and swimming my pony in the Warrandyte river, picking apples off the trees while Chiquita ate windfalls from the ground.

One afternoon I went down to the paddock but couldn't find Chiquita in the usual place. I followed the creek halfway along and eventually saw her standing under a tree. She didn't come when I called her. As I got closer, I saw her near-side front leg jammed in the fork of a tree by the banks of the creek. She must have slipped in the mud and got her front leg jammed deeper and deeper as she tried to get out. My heart sank. She stood very still, knowing I was trying to help her, but I couldn't budge her leg. Tears streaming down my face, I ran to the SEC depot where some of the workers were just finishing up. Three of them came down to the creek and somehow got her out, but her leg was badly damaged. She was in a lot of pain and couldn't put her foot to the ground. I ran up to the phone box near home and called a vet. He said it looked as though she'd been there most of the day, cutting off the circulation. The tendons would probably contract. He did what he could for her, and showed me how to massage and exercise the leg and hoof. I did that for a couple of weeks, but the tendons contracted, the hoof folded under and she started hobbling on the front of her pastern, which soon became red raw, then ulcerated.

Jack and Nan spoke to me about this, telling me we couldn't leave Chiquita in pain any longer – she wasn't going to get better and had to be put down. I had no option. I agreed. I knew that day she wouldn't be there when I got home from school, but at the same time I didn't believe it. I didn't want to believe it. And when my parents offered me the money from the dog-meat man, I screamed and threw it back at them. I hated them both. I hated life.

I spent three days and nights wandering through paddocks in a daze, patting other people's horses, but not riding them. I wouldn't talk to anyone, I wouldn't eat, and I cried so much I thought my ribs were going to snap.

The grief was almost unbearable. I didn't care about anything or anyone, and I was starting to 'float' mentally. This is a strange sensation I get that I now recognise as being a symptom of dissociation, a state in which time does not exist. I think it is a defence-mechanism I developed early in life – one that came back to me many years later when I was sentenced to death; not grieving for myself, but for the man I had killed.

I eventually went back to school after Chiquita was put down, but my marks went right down. I started hanging around with a girl called Wendy. She was big, had black hair, wore leathers and rode a motorbike to school. She taught me how to smoke. We accidentally started a grass fire at the back of the school when we were supposed to be sitting a French exam. I guess the only thing we had in common was that neither of us wanted to be there.

Most of the girls in my class were one or two years older than me because I had been fast-tracked for good results in primary school. These girls were experimenting with make-up, buying nice clothes to wear to dances and flirting with boys. A few, I remember, got pregnant.

I was screwing with a tow-truck driver at the time, but never got pregnant. My mother asked me to bring him home so she could meet him. He came around to the house one afternoon when she was drinking and they had a good long chat while I was outside. He came around again with a friend of his, at night, when I was already in bed.

To my amazement she let them come into my room and sit on my bed. I can't remember what we talked about, but I knew something strange was going on. As it turned out, the tow-truck driver ended up being the first of three of my 'boyfriends' Nan chatted up. She used me as bait to find young lovers for herself.

Meanwhile, Eric was trying to sell me to a friend of his across the road in return for cigarettes. His friend was a nice quiet person, clean-cut, a good Catholic in every way. He must have wanted to practise having sex without getting into trouble, and Eric struck up a deal with him without telling me. He just said his friend wanted to take me for a drive in his car on the weekend. We ended up driving all over the countryside, then into town, around near the MCG. There had been a bit of small talk, not much, then silence. He was sweating and uncomfortable. It suddenly dawned on me what the problem was.

'Did Eric say I would screw with you?' I asked.

'No, no – well, yes.'

There was a long silence. I couldn't help him. At only twelve years old I didn't know how to seduce a man. Eventually he said he didn't think it was a good idea and we drove home. But Eric still screwed me when it suited him. I grew up thinking this was normal behaviour – but no one talked about it.

CHAPTER 4

Leaving Home

About halfway through 1965, when I was fourteen, my mother decided to run away from home.

I didn't know she was planning to go. I arrived home from school one afternoon and found the back door open. It was usually locked, the house empty. But when the back door was open I knew she would be inside, sitting at the kitchen table, drinking herself into a rage over something or nothing. Normally I would have run to the front of the house, peeked in through the kitchen window and counted how many big brown empties she had lined up. If it was more than five or six she would be well on her way to a violent outburst, in which case I would duck away and escape to the old quarry, or to the creek, or to any number of orchards which I then knew like the back of my hand. These 'hideouts', as I called them, were safe because my mother didn't like getting mud on her shoes. She was fastidious about outward appearances and cleanliness. And although she had chased me in the past, she preferred to play a waiting game. If I wasn't in the house by nightfall she would lock me out until I was so cold and hungry I would plead to be let in. Once inside, I was systematically flogged then sent to bed with no tea. That was the pattern until I was about eleven years old. As I grew bigger, the floggings decreased. They were replaced with the silent treatment (which didn't make much difference), and with not being allowed out of the house, which was the worst punishment I could get. However, in order to keep me inside the house for any length of time my mother had to stay there too, so these situations always ended up a stalemate – until the next time she decided to 'teach me a lesson'.

On this afternoon I was apprehensive, but didn't run. Something was different this time, so I took my shoes off and went inside.

'I want to talk to you,' she said. I sat at the opposite side of the table, facing her, waiting for whatever was coming.

'How would you like to come and live with me in the city? Just you and me. I'm leaving Jack, and I want you to come with me.' I wasn't game to ask why she wanted to take me with her. She had a glazed look in her eyes and her chin was thrust forward, her jaw clenched, a sign that she was hoarding her anger, waiting to hurl it at the first person who crossed her.

'What about Edd and Dan?' I asked softly.

'The boys can stay with Jack.'

'What about school? I'm not old enough to leave.'

'I've arranged all that.' Just how well she had 'arranged all that' I would find out later. At the time I only knew that once she had arranged something, I could not say no. She was asking me to make a choice, but also letting me know I had no choice.

'Yes,' I said, eyes down. 'When are we going?'

'Tomorrow. Early!'

And that was that. She turned away to stare out the window. The conversation was over. She would save her verbal violence for

Jack when he came home from work – and hurt him all the more by telling him I wanted to go with her.

With a suitcase each and frying pan, we shifted to Clifton Hill, one of the old inner-city suburbs of Melbourne close to Carlton where, incidentally, I was born. We moved into a terrace house, two streets back from the main road and tramway into town. I remember the cement footpath wet from recent rain, the rusting cast-iron gate that let out a screeching sound as my mother pushed it open, the peeling paint on the wood-panelled door at the front of the house, and once inside, a long dark passageway. The narrowness of this terrace house always gave me the feeling I was entering an underground tunnel: it was dark, damp and depressing. At the other end of the tunnel was a small backyard. There was no lawn or garden, just dirt and gravel, a few clumps of weeds, an outhouse, and an old clothesline on a wooden prop, all of which was surrounded by a huge brick wall with one small access gate to the back lane. This brick wall blocked all vision. It had chunks of broken bricks and glass cemented along the top of it, and two strands of barbed wire attached to metal pegs above that. Having just come from what my mother called 'the bush', I had never seen anything like it. It was a monstrosity that made me feel unsafe rather than safe. It made me feel locked up and since there was nothing of value on the property I could not work out what it was supposed to be safeguarding. I had no idea that we might be unsafe in our new home.

My mother didn't bother to tell me initially that Carlton and Clifton Hill were rough areas, but she did warn me about the park at the end of our street. 'Don't hang around in the park,' she said. 'People have been killed in there.' My imagination ran wild with images I had seen on television: shadowy men dragging blood-soaked bodies behind trees, then slinking off into the darkness or merging into an anonymous crowd on the city streets. For a few days I was scared. But I soon found I preferred being in the park to being in the house, and I went there often. For although there was the noise of city traffic nearby to get used to, I was comforted by the familiar feel of bark, the smell of grass and earth, the sound of crunching autumn leaves in my hand. Not many other people used the park, and I was glad to have it to myself. I would sit for long hours under a tree imagining I was Maid Marion, and that the good guy, Robin Hood, would rescue me from my mother and her love of city life. I had seen Robin Hood on television, had liked his band of merry men and the way they always out-foxed the Sheriff of Nottingham. The good guys always won on television, things always turned out right, and I took that to be a formula for life: if I was 'good' enough, things would turn out right for me.

Nan often stayed in the city long after she had finished work. She wanted to 'enjoy life', as she put it, and even though I knew she didn't, the message she sent out was that she could enjoy it more without me around. On the occasions when she was at home, there was no laughter in our house. And no conversation, of course. But there was music. As she sat at the kitchen table, drowning her sorrows, she would play Gershwin's *Porgy and Bess*: 'I Got Plenty of Nothin', 'Summertime', and 'Bess... You Is My Woman Now'.

Sometimes I would lie on my bed soaking up these mournful songs and working myself into a morbid state. I used to cry into my pillow, trying to smother the noise (because my mother got angry when I cried), and not having a clue as to why I was miserable. On one level I sensed that I was making myself miserable, but I also knew that crying would bring relief, that the exhaustion of crying would bring sleep. Sometimes I needed that. Most of the time, though, I needed to get out of the house, out of the dark and into the light, so

I was pleased when I was told I would be starting work soon.

Nan arranged a job for me at Foys, the city department store where she worked. How she 'arranged' this, I don't know. I was not only under the school leaving age, but I was also socially backward and not very good with figures or money. I suppose she told them I was a good worker, which I was. I learnt to put a lot of effort into working hard because that was one of the few ways by which I could please or appease other people. So there I was, a 'young adult' working in haberdashery at one of the biggest department stores in Melbourne.

I went to work dressed in some of Nan's old clothes: a yellowing white blouse, a tight black skirt, and a pair of black pointy-toe stilettos. I had never worn heels before and the stilettos were awkward to stand in for any length of time, and when I walked in them I had to lean my top half forward and stick my back half out in order to balance. The tight skirt shortened my stride like a pair of knee-hobbles, and I was embarrassed when people stared at me. I was earning £4 2s 6p a week. I had to pay my mother £2 a week board, and out of the rest buy food, clothes and toiletries, and keep enough for fares. My money didn't go very far. I began to resent paying board because my mother spent it on booze. She was forever complaining that she didn't have enough money, but she always seemed to have enough for beer and cigarettes.

I couldn't spend much time in the park during the winter months because there was no shelter. I was glad when spring came around, bringing with it new foliage on the trees and warm breezes which gave me a wonderful feeling of well-being. I was restless, though; city life was a lonely life for me at the age of fourteen.

I did have a 'boyfriend' for a while. His name was Ray. He was one of the SEC linesmen who had helped get Chiquita out of the tree fork. When I had gone down to the creek to dress her wounded leg and do the stretching exercises, Ray would come down to see how we were getting on. Before long we started having sex. At that time I was thirteen. He was 21. We went in his car to his parents' place sometimes. He had a collection of Buddy Holly records which we listened to while having sex in a spare room. Ray wasn't very nice to his parents and not much nicer to me. He never took me to the drive-in, or to a dance – the usual thing young people did in those days. He just came around for sex, and lost interest in that after my mother seduced him.

One afternoon when I was home on my own at Clifton Hill, Ray knocked on the door. I was surprised to see him, but didn't ask how he knew where we lived. He was the third of my boyfriends Nan 'stole' from me. The second was a young mechanic who liked to play cricket. He used to take me out a lot, but didn't want sex. A year or so later I found out why. I caught him with my mother when I came home unexpectedly.

One Saturday afternoon I was down in the park eating fish and chips and idly reading the newspaper's employment classifieds. I wasn't qualified for any of the jobs, but unwrapped the page around the flake and potato cakes and read on. I tried to imagine myself in these other lives, but I couldn't get the mind pictures to flow. I couldn't relate to those other worlds.

Then I saw it: 'Young person wanted for dairy farm, prefer female, experience not necessary…' I was ecstatic. Wow! What joy! Freedom! I could hardly believe it. There it was, in black and white – a job for me. 'Please God, please,' I prayed as I ran up the hill to ask my mother for permission to leave Foys, to work on a farm in the country. I felt sure that if she said yes, my future happiness would be guaranteed.

Nan said she would think about it. I was amazed my mother would even consider letting me go, but she did, and one day took me for an interview with the farmer's wife. Like a concerned parent, she quizzed the woman about work and living conditions. Apparently they wanted a female who would do housework and farm work. I agreed enthusiastically.

'It won't be all spring lambs and daisies you know,' warned the farmer's wife, who was heavily pregnant. 'Yes, I know,' I beamed at her – not knowing, not caring, for my mind was full of dreams and was capable of totally ignoring unpleasant distractions imposed on it by others. I didn't want to know about the harsh realities of farm life; I just wanted to be free. My idea of freedom then was being close to nature, out in the rain, covered in mud, wearing jeans and gumboots and a tatty old shirt, being messy, dishevelled, sober – everything my mother was not.

I watched my mother making the big decision, prolonging my anxiety and unsettling the farmer's wife.

She sat with her legs crossed like a *Vogue* model, her back very straight and her chin titled slightly upwards. She was affecting elegant puffs on her Coles cigarette-holder, blowing long streams of smoke up to the ceiling through rounded, re-painted lips. My mother was an actress when she thought she had an audience, and on that day she was playing Greta Garbo: strong, elegant, enigmatic. She might have been thinking, 'I want to be alone' as she at last agreed to let me go. I was so happy. I felt such gratitude. For a while I almost liked my mother.

I travelled down to San Remo by car with the farmer's wife. San Remo is a narrow strip of land jutting out from the Victorian mainland, leading to Phillip Island. If you were to draw a cross-section of the area, there would be a bay on the northern side, a highway, a steep hill of farmland rising to the south and levelling off, sheer cliffs, and then the ocean, Bass Straight. It was a small farm, about 80 hectares carrying 120 milkers when the calving had finished. When I arrived there, the grass in the paddocks was nearly a foot high and very thick. But it was also water-logged, so I learnt, and the cows had to be supplemented with hay at that time of the year.

The couple I worked for were share-farmers. My first impression of their house was of a weather-beaten, weatherboard box stuck out in the middle of a paddock. Nearby was a dam, further over the dairy and hay sheds, and further still, in the distance, was the owner's house. It was a large brick and tile house with a smoking chimney, and was surrounded by tall pines and a thick hedge. I never met the owner of the farm. I saw him a couple of times heading over the hill on his new red tractor, being chased by my boss on his old grey Ferguson. My boss called him 'a gentleman farmer', and I gathered from the sneering tone of this remark that there was bad business between them.

My boss worked very hard, and so did I. It was my job to bring the cows in first thing in the morning. It was freezing cold, and I had to walk out into the darkness and mud with only a small torch to light my way. I could hear the sea crashing onto the cliffs at the back of the farm, and it was eerie until I got used to it. As soon as I opened the gate to whatever paddock the cows were in at the time, they made their own way down to the dairy, mooing softly and intermittently, then more loudly and continuously if I had forgotten to open the bottom gate into the yards. I was glad they knew their own way around, because they were big cows and I was afraid of the ones with horns when I couldn't see them in the dark.

The washing of udders and application of cups was easy

enough, even with six bails in operation at once. But when it came to looking after the vat and associated apparatus, I often made mistakes. My boss explained the procedure for dismantling, cleaning, and reconnecting all the bits and pieces once, expecting me to remember it all from then on. However, I didn't have a good memory for mechanical things. Sometimes I forgot to close the outlet valve on the vat and the milk would run out from under the dairy door and flow into the manure-spattered cement holding yard. As soon as I saw that white river spread out through the delta of cow dung, I wanted to die. 'What the…! What the heck…!' my boss would shout, running off to fix the vat. Then he would storm back out again, yelling. 'Do you know how much this is costing me? Do you?!' until it was time for me to hose and scrape the yards. It took me quite a while to learn how to use the squeegee without spraying watery green manure all over myself. My slowness in cleaning the yards caused the boss to shout at me again, 'Time is money!', and he seemed to be a very hard man. But as soon as we left the dairy for breakfast he would be in a good mood again.

After breakfast we loaded up the trailer with hay to feed out. Some of the cows were calving, and hid their calves in clumps of reeds, so we had to go slowly to avoid running over them. For the first week the boss drove the tractor, and I threw out chunks of hay as we went along. Then he decided that I should drive while he fed out hay.

'But I don't know how to drive,' I said.

'Well I'll show you. This is the accelerator, this is the clutch, this is the brake, this is first, this is second, and this is top. You have to double the clutch. Right?'

I didn't have a clue what a clutch was, or what 'first', 'second', and 'top' referred to, but thought I'd give it a go. Luckily he had the good sense to start me off on fairly level ground, for I never really knew what gear I was in or how to slow the thing down. 'Whoa! Whoa! Too fast! Sto-o-o-o-pp!' he shouted from the trailer as we hurtled towards a fence or a gate. When I became more proficient I was sent out to feed hay on my own. On one unusually wet day I ended up doing a roller-coaster down a very slippery track, panicked, slammed the brakes on, slid sideways through the gateway, and narrowly missed wiping out the side of the hay shed.

I often had an hour or two off between lunch and the afternoon milking. I had to do the dishes, wash the toddler's nappies – left with all their contents in the bath – and sweep. Then I would take off, feeling free and gloriously happy. On warm dry days I walked all over the farm, as far away from the house as possible. I spent a lot of time lying on my back out in the paddocks, shutting the rest of the world out of my thoughts. There was a pony on the farm that I was allowed to ride, although I soon discovered riding him was not a relaxing way to spend the afternoon. He was a fat pony, comfortable enough to ride bareback, but if he spotted any leftover hay in some distant corner of a paddock he would throw his head up, grab the bit and bolt towards it. When he reached the hay he put his head down and propped, invariably throwing me over his neck to the ground. He wouldn't run off, but I couldn't get him to budge until he'd eaten every last snippet of that hay.

One day I rode him to the cliffs at the back of the farm. I wanted to have a close look at Shelley Bay, a crescent-shaped bay at the bottom of the cliffs covered in shells and only accessible when the tide was out. I tied the pony up to a bush, climbed down the cliffs, and began fossicking on the beach. I was so fascinated by the shells and driftwood that I completely forgot the time – until a wave crashed onto my legs, filled my boots, and nearly sucked me out to sea as it receded. Being a Victorian I had heard stories of our southern coast, of people who were sucked into underwater caves and never seen again. When the wave hit me I remembered these stories, and I panicked. My gumboots were half buried in wet sand, and another wave was approaching. In fact the tide was coming in very quickly. I realised I might not have time to get back to the cliffs. I ran barefoot, my heart pounding. Shells were cutting my feet. Waves were crashing in, racing towards me. I was very frightened. I reached the cliffs alright, then couldn't find the path I had climbed down. Shadows moved, everything looked different, but I kept on searching for a way out.

When I did find the path and climbed, nearly exhausted, to the top, the pony was gone. I started walking. After some ten minutes I found him, but every time I got within reach of the reins he took off again. Half an hour passed before he let me catch him again, and as soon as I had hold of him I did a mean thing. I hit him angrily on the neck, venting my fear and frustration on a pony whose only interests were eating and playing chasey. I was very subdued for the rest of that day, realising for the first time that I was mortal.

My job on the farm seemed fairly secure until the day I 'lost' the tractor. I'd been harrowing a front paddock on the west side of the farm when I stopped about halfway up the hill and got off to shift an old log. I was trying to roll the log down the hill, without much luck. Meantime, the tractor rolled down the hill, harrows clanking behind, straight through the fence and into a deep ditch between the road and the fence. This time the boss stayed very angry.

I'd also been having trouble with one of 'my' cows, whose large and low teats were cracked from dragging in the clay mud around the dam. I tried to dodge her at milking because her teats were sore and she kicked when I went to put the cups on. Even when I leg-roped her she managed to kick the cups out of my hand with the other leg. She must have known I was scared of her because she was not quite so difficult when the boss took over. The morning after the tractor incident he insisted I milk that cow.

'Either you milk this cow, or I'll get someone else who will,' was his ultimatum. Whether his words were a bluff or a real threat, I'll never know. My reaction at the time was a strong feeling of not being wanted anymore. I clammed up, refused to talk, left the cow standing in the yard, and went over to the hayshed to cry. That was the only way I knew how to deal with the perceived threat; it didn't occur to me to discuss the matter with my boss, or to ask for his help, because I hadn't those social skills and felt intimidated by his anger.

About an hour later I saw the family drive out the front gate, going to church. Having already decided to run away, I saw this as the perfect opportunity to 'escape'. I had no idea that, as an employed person, I could terminate my own employment and ask for my pay.

As soon as they were out of sight I ran over to the house, packed my one small suitcase, and took off. There were no trees or bushes to hide behind along that coastal strip, so every time I heard a car coming I jumped down into the ditch along the side of the road. When I reached the highway I felt free again, although only from the immediate past. Where would I go? The only thing I could think of was to go back to my mother. I feared my mother also, but at least that was a familiar fear. Whether running away from her or running back to her, it was still a sign of her domination over me.

CHAPTER 5

Rape and Reform

I hitchhiked back to Melbourne. My next memory is of being on a train, heading out to where Nan lived. I stayed at her new place for a while, but I couldn't get a job. Looking back on it, though, I didn't try very hard. Each 'rejection' threw me into a fit of useless despair, and I would stay in bed for days, trying to sleep my life away. Nan didn't seem to care; she went off to work as usual, and when at home pretended nothing was wrong.

She started walking the streets at night. It crossed my mind she might be on the game, prostituting herself. But I soon discounted the idea. She was off the grog, and had nothing to replace her late-night drinking habits with. I went with her one night. She was in a stormy silent mood, her high heels snapping savagely on the cement footpath.

'Where are we going?' I asked, almost breathless, trying to keep up with her.

'To the ocean.' I can only guess now that she saw the ocean symbolically, that she got some comfort from being near the sea.

She walked on, but as the ocean was three kilometres away, I turned back.

She

When my mother was suicidal
she would walk to the sea
for miles, high-heels click-clacking
savagely on cement footpaths;
refusing to talk, she would walk off
into the dismal night
and we never knew whether she
might really 'do it' this time.
I grew up believing my mother
had a pact with the sea,
that sooner or later it would claim her.

As an adult I have learnt to love
the sea: salt winds, yellow sands,
white shells and cuttlefish,
me running, laughing, swimming out,
catching/riding waves rushing in;
and from an island with friends
rowing out in an old wooden boat
to a favourite spot
where we stop, safely secured –
where lapping water rocks me,
carries me back on waves of emotion
far beyond childhood fear.

Greenough Regional Prison, 21 March 1993

I'm not sure how many times Nan attempted suicide, but we all grew up with her threats and those mysterious trips to the hospital. Suicide was a way of life for our mother, and the emotional blackmail that accompanied it was a way of life for us.

Now we were shifting again, from Mordialloc into a pub in the city. I was now about fifteen. Nan was spending a lot more time at Micky Powell's Dance Studios, just up the street from the pub. She'd taught there on a part-time basis for years, at one stage taking me along on Saturday afternoons for lessons. I never felt comfortable there but my mother loved the old-time dance music, the make-up and the hairspray, the ball gowns and glittering shoes. Most of all she loved to be in control of other people, which on the dance floor she was. I didn't mind the dancing too much, but hated the artificiality of the whole scene. I preferred the smell of horse manure to that of strong perfume and hairspray. After working on the dairy farm, this idea became even stronger in my mind, and my mother gave up trying to make a 'lady' out of me after that.

I walked all over Melbourne looking for work. I applied at a coffee shop that had a 'Waitress Wanted' sign in the window. The owner said I could start in a few days, but would have to prove I was a good worker before he would pay me. I worked there for a week, polishing, cleaning, filling up the shelves with stock, serving coffee and cake. On the Friday afternoon he told me I was not suitable and would have to finish up – without pay. This was his rort; the sign in the window never came down, and he already had someone lined up to take my place. With my usual self-blaming thoughts, I blamed myself for getting ripped off. But I also knew I had done a good job, which gave me the confidence to try again.

I was soon employed, and paid, by an old couple who owned a

lunch bar. They didn't talk much, but instructed me carefully on food preparation: melt the butter for thinner spreading on sandwiches; ice up the milk so it froths higher in milkshakes, using less milk; slice the tomatoes paper thin, one slice per sandwich; don't change the dishwater too often, it wastes detergent, and so on. It was a popular place, always packed over the lunch hour.

One day I asked the woman what the tattoo was along the inside of her lower arm. She gave me a long, deep sort of look, but said nothing. In a strange coincidence, I went to one of the city's numerous matinees – my city 'hideouts' – the next weekend and saw a movie about a female spy who was sent to a concentration camp. It was a second-rate move, more like a horror show, which I didn't usually like to watch. The reason I stayed to see this one through was that the Nazis tattooed a number on the heroine's arm when she was first sent to the camp – the same sort of number both my employers had. I realised they were holocaust Jews... their strange accent... their obsession with not wasting anything... it all made sense. I felt very close to them then, or at least, closer than I did to anyone else at the time.

I was happy working for the old couple. They never got angry with me, and gave me a free lunch every workday. I also liked them because they didn't ask a lot of questions. As long as I was doing my work, they were content to live for the day without prying into the past. I wanted to save enough money to buy some new clothes, and one day get a place of my own to live in. But those things were not to be.

Taking My Mother Home

She lurched down city streets,
swaying heavily,

leaning on me
in night's dark spaces,
attempting to stand
when people passed,
when light revealed our deformity.
An accident of birth
bound me to her,
so when she fell and skidded
on knee and outstretched palm,
lay there retching,
I too felt ill:
her shame was my shame
as I became
the mother of the child.

Greenough Regional Prison, 1994

Nan was drinking again. She sent me out with one of her drunken friends from the pub one night. It was obvious she wanted to get rid of me for the night.

'Now you look after my little girl,' she said to him, half stung, through the smoke-haze of the crowded lounge.

He took me to another pub, two blocks down, and ordered a beer for each of us. There was some question about my age, an argument followed, and we left. 'Let's go for a walk,' he said, angry, but trying to sound pleasant. We walked back up the street, past the dance studio, and up to a park at the edge of the city square. As we crossed the road and entered the park, I began to relax. Parks were my most comfortable places in the city, although I didn't usually sit in them at night.

As we walked into the park, I looked for somewhere to sit. A park bench, away from city noise, haloes of mist around the park lights, a nice place to rest and talk.

'Your mother tells me you're a good root.'

'No, I'm not!'

'She says you've been at it a long time?'

Silence from me.

'Come on love,' he said, sliming up to me, breathing beer in my face, 'How do you reckon your mum got her drinking money tonight?'

I tried to run, but he threw me to the ground. 'No,' I screamed, 'Get off.' But he was too strong. I remember his whiskers scratching my face, his chest crushing mine, his hand clawing at me and eventually him grunting like a pig. As soon as he penetrated me, I stopped struggling. When it was over he just walked away and left me there. I don't know how long I stayed on the ground. I went into a sort of trance; I couldn't cry, think, feel or move. I just lay there.

At some time early in the morning, the police found me wandering down the street. My dress was torn near one shoulder, not much, and was wet from where I had been lying on the ground. I was shivering, but not from cold; my nerves had gone haywire. When the police questioned me, I wouldn't talk to them. I felt as though I was being interrogated, as though I was being accused of doing something wrong. Also, having grown up being constantly told to shut up, that's exactly what I did when I felt threatened. My silence was both an obedience and a self-defence.

Down at the police station they questioned me again. When I still wouldn't talk they sent a female officer in, who nearly tipped me off my chair. 'I'm in no mood for his sort of shit,' she said. She was angry, so I gave her my name and address. Then I was left on my own, until two officers came in with my mother. 'She's uncontrollable!' she yelled at them, ignoring me as though I wasn't in the room. 'I've tried my best, but she just won't listen!'

I don't know what else was said that night. I only know that I was sent to court, was charged with 'being a neglected child', and locked up in a reformatory. As to the rape, it wasn't a case of me losing my virginity. I had lost that when I was four or five years old, and been screwed ever since. What mattered to me was that for the first time I had fought it, tried to say no, but couldn't. I hated that man, I hated my mother, I hated myself. I went into a deep depression.

Winlaton was a notorious 'girl's home' or reformatory in Melbourne, a place where 'all the bad girls go'. Several officers accused me of having been on drugs because I wouldn't get out of bed on time and spent all the recreation time sleeping on the floor. Actually, it's my habit to curl up on the floor (or ground) with one arm over my face when I'm depressed. I don't move for hours, and probably look as though I'm asleep. I just wanted to be left alone, but they won't let you withdraw, or die, in places like that. There was a strict routine which had to be adhered to. I can't remember all of it now, only that eating, sleeping, working and playing were all ordered by a bell and followed up by bullying officers. No one could be late for anything. Talking was only allowed at certain times, in certain places. And cleanliness was 'next to godliness'.

We had to line up for showers early in the morning, under strict supervision, and each girl had exactly two minutes to wash. As one stepped out, another stepped in. It was freezing waiting for a shower, and if the hot water ran out by the time your turn came around, that was too bad – you had a cold shower.

Within a week I was given a job in the kitchen, scrubbing floors after the cooks had finished. The floor was painted a sky-blue colour, and all scuff marks had to be scrubbed off. One afternoon as I was on my hands and knees, soaping up the floor with a scrubbing-brush, music from a radio was playing nearby. I wasn't taking much notice until a song by the Righteous Brothers came on:

> *The sun ain't gonna shine any more,*
> *The moon ain't gonna rise in the sky,*
> *When you're withou-out love…*

I was so upset by this song that I forgot about not crying out loud. I cried so hard that I was gasping for breath, my chest was aching, and my whole body shook violently. I felt so weak that I couldn't even sit up, so ended up rolling around in the soap suds, wailing loudly, until I wore myself out.

I didn't think things could get much worse, but they did. One afternoon after sport – which I did not participate in – I wandered over to a grassy slope near the back of the section. No one missed me when the girls were taken back in. I wasn't thinking about going over the wire, just lying face-down in the late afternoon sun and breathing in the wonderful smell of grass. The next thing my name was being called, officers were running towards me, and I was carted off 'up top'.

'Up top' was punishment section, a long red brick building with bars on the windows. I was put in solitary, a bare brick cell with a metal bed-frame bolted to the wall and floor, and some meagre bedding folded at one end of the bed. All the girls up top had one of these single cells, but were only 'in solitary' when they were not allowed out for recreation.

After three or four days I was let out for 'recreation'. The recreation room was adjacent to the block office, and there was a plate-glass window nearly the size of one wall between the two rooms. We could be observed at any time, and were observed nearly all the time. There was no furniture in the room; about 10 of us just sat around on the floor, leaning against the walls for up to three hours at a time, and that was our recreation.

The girls up top were known as the 'tough' girls. Most of them had tattoos all over them, and their favourite occupation was applying more tattoos to themselves and each other. This was a tricky business because needles and ink had to be stolen and smuggled in, and because tattooing was a chargeable offence. One day I put some on my lower arm – a highly visible place. Ironically, I tattooed myself with the names of two people I disliked and feared the most, my mother and my older brother.

One girl was literally covered in tattoos, including on her face, and she used to swallow needles so that she would have to be taken to hospital. The first time this happened, she escaped, so the next time they left her until she was in agony before taking her to town. She kept swallowing needles though. When I asked her why she said, 'I'm not going to let the bastards beat me.' This girl had grown up the hard way on the streets of Fitzroy, saw life as a running battle against the police and anyone else who tried to tie her down. On one level I was in awe of her, but on another felt sorry for her. I could tell she wasn't happy.

Life up top was worse than no life at all. Time went very slowly for me, especially when my mother left messages she would be in on the weekend for a visit. I would wait all week for the weekend, then wait all weekend for the visit, in vain. A few weeks later she would turn up unexpectedly and act as though nothing had happened. My feelings started to swing wildly: I still hated her, but I desperately wanted to see her. I thought she could get me out, just give the order or make a request and take me home. But it became obvious after a while that she was enjoying life without me. 'There's a new man in my life,' she informed me one time, babbling on like a teenager about her, her plans, and her feelings. I knew then that she was going to leave me locked up. For how long, I didn't know. Maybe years. One of the other girls had told me the state could keeps us wards until we were 21. I couldn't bear the thought of it. I lost hope, had nothing to look forward to, gave up.

One thing about being at the end of the line is that you can't be pushed any further. When solitary confinement and loss of visits is used as punishment, there's not much else they can do when you refuse to come out of your cell and refuse visits. They can drag you to the showers, but then they have to wash you like a baby – and they don't like getting their uniforms wet. I was labelled 'uncooperative' and sent to see the psychologist.

'They tell me you haven't been eating regularly, or mixing with the other girls. Is that right?' I said nothing.

'Well perhaps you can tell me what the problem is... maybe I can help?' I still said nothing. What was the point? She went on and on, perhaps this, and perhaps that, persistently probing and penetrating, getting through my defences. Eventually she wore me down.

'I hate my mother,' I said, tears welling. 'I want to go home to my father and brothers.'

'I'm afraid that's out of the question, my dear. You will not be allowed to return to your stepfather for such time as you remain a ward of the state.'

'What!? Why not?'

'Your mother has some kind of medical evidence, I believe, that he was interfering with you.'

I clammed up. Mind racing, I searched the past for some kind of connection. Not Jack, I thought, not my father! You idiots. It was Eric screwing me all those years... and others. But not Dad, he's not like that. How did she...? Hang on... ahh, the medical examination, that's right. She said I had to be checked by a doctor before I could start using tampons, to see if it was safe. And I believed her. She must have got a certificate to say I was not a virgin, and then blamed Jack for it. So that's how she 'managed' to get me an exemption from school. Special circumstances, I bet she said. But why didn't anyone ask me? No one ever asks me.

I don't know how long I sat there until the psychologist's voice broke into my consciousness again. She was going on about something or other.

'What?'

'I said, what do you want to do with your life?'

'I want to sit out in a paddock under a tree,' I replied sullenly.

She drew herself up straight, stared hard at me, then rose and went to open the door. I started to leave, but the superintendent was standing there. The psychologist beamed a sickly-sweet smile at the superintendent, and in her carefully cultivated voice said, 'She wants to sit under a tree.' They both stared at me as though I was a weird aberration of the species.

Two or three weeks later I was called up again, this time to the superintendent's office. She was all right, the super. I used to clean her apartment windows when I was down in the other section, and she was one person I felt I could relax with. When I went into her office that day, she asked me to sit down. She was looking very pleased with herself.

'How would you like to work on a farm in the country?'

I was dumbstruck.

'It's a fairly large wheat and sheep property up in central Victoria,' she went on. 'The three girls of the family are away at boarding school, and there is an opening for someone to groom and exercise their horses, clean the stables, things like that. We have made enquiries on your behalf, and the job is yours... if you want it. What do you say?'

I was overcome with emotion. Instant tears ran down my cheeks, dripped off my chin like raindrops off guttering after a sudden storm. I wanted to run around the big desk to hug her, to tell her how wonderful she was, but I couldn't move or speak. She sat there patiently, waiting for the tears to pass, until eventually I managed a thin, croaky 'Thank you.' I could hope again. The sun -was going to shine again, shine on me. I walked trance-like back to my cell, not excited, but deeply grateful to someone or something for what was, to me, a new lease on life.

CHAPTER 6

Travels

The government bought me some new clothes for the job. In my suitcase there were fleecy cotton shirts, two pair of jeans, a long nightie, a new jumper, toothbrush, toothpaste and soap, some hankies, three pair of socks – and a pair of gumboots. I loved those gumboots.

Arrangements had been made for me to travel up to Wedderburn by train. As I was being taken to the train, I didn't feel any of the anticipation I had felt when I was leaving for the farm at San Remo. Being in an institution had a negative effect on me. My body and mind was intact, but my spirit was crushed. When I went through the gate, back into the world, I felt as though only half of me was going: one half was getting on with living and working, the other half was still locked up. People on the outside were no longer just anonymous, they were alien. My experience was another language, one that could not be translated or shared. That feeling of alienation remained with me for many years.

I remember the train ride well. It was an old train which had wood panelling and leather upholstery inside. The small windows could be opened with an upward push, letting the air rush in and the scenery rush by before my watering eyes. When it got too cold, I shut the window again. The rocking motion of the train and constant clacking of the wheels was comforting. I enjoyed the feeling of being carried along, like a leaf on a surging river, only this 'river' of steel was carrying me inland, not to the sea. We passed many small farms, lush green paddocks with tumble-down sheds and flood-ravaged fences. Weeping willows and huge old river-gums which had stood the test of time were prominent features of the landscape during the first stage of the trip. But these were gradually replaced by thinner gums, by 'the bush' as inland Victorians know it. As we headed into the edge of the wheat belt, the land became flatter and the scenery more monotonous. It was all heaven to me, though.

I wondered what the girls would be like. I felt sure they would be posh and snotty, simply because they went to boarding school. As it turned out, the farmer's daughters were quite down to earth and accepted me very well. When they came home for the holidays, they seemed to be intent on enjoying their freedom from the restrictions of school: shopping, riding, tennis, mustering sheep when it was necessary. We were riding out one day when we met some 'gypsies' with an old ute and a caravan. They were driving sheep along the road verges. The girls called them gypsies, but they were probably just poor farmers or contractors. They had some good working dogs which kept the sheep off the road for the most part, but they were moving slowly, letting the sheep eat along the way. I was fascinated. What a life! I'd have given anything to join them, having romantic visions of boiling the billy at sunset, of wandering the countryside forever without a care; but I was a ward of the state and had to go where I was told.

The girls' mother was a nice woman, always baking, washing, ironing or gardening. The father was a gruff man, though. He was the boss of the family; no one dared interrupt him or answer back when he spoke. I felt that he didn't like me, and I was afraid of him. More than anything, I was afraid to ask for my pay. After months of work, I had not been paid. His wife sometimes whispered to me while we were doing the dishes, 'You should ask for your pay this week. You're entitled to it, you know.' But I was always too afraid to ask.

One day, after the girls had gone back to school, he was having trouble running the horses in from a nearby paddock. Instead of following him and the farmhand, I cut across the paddock and blocked the horses between some trees and the fence. He was very pleased with me, praising my 'initiative' at the lunch table. Good, I thought, maybe he is pleased enough to pay me now. But he didn't. On reflection, I think he might have wanted to teach me to be assertive, to stand up for my rights, but I didn't know then that I had any rights, and I was easily intimidated.

I was exercising one of the horses along the lanes that surrounded the paddocks one afternoon when the boss drove up behind me. The horse was a cunning one that shied badly when taken out on his own. I didn't know then how to correct that sort of habit, so it was really a case of the horse taking me for a ride rather than the other way around. When the boss drove up the horse shied violently, slammed me up against a tree, then tried to take off. Luckily I was able to stay on and pull him up. But the boss blasted me: 'Don't you know anything about horses!? I thought you said you could ride...' Then he revved the ute furiously and left, leaving a long cloud of dust for me to choke on. I'd been feeling down anyway that afternoon, and was unable to take his criticism. I translated it into a total rejection; and in what was to become another pattern in my life, I rejected him in turn. I kept on riding away from the farm, not knowing where I was going, knowing only that I was not going to hang around for any more verbal abuse. I rode on for miles, thinking of the Lone Ranger, who said 'Hi-ho Silver' then galloped off over the horizon in television's perpetual happy endings. I could not understand why my life was full of unhappy endings.

When I stopped daydreaming and thought about the situation realistically, I didn't know what to do next. I was worried about the police catching me and sending me back to Winlaton. On the other hand, I knew Australia was a big country; if I could run fast enough and far enough, the police would never catch me. I was a good worker. I could get another job in the bush, stay there until I was 21... or forever. 'Forever' was one of my daydream words, but somehow it got mixed up in my vision of reality, of how my ideal reality should be. I couldn't see that I was running away from reality: I thought I was running towards it.

I rode back late at night, put the horse in his stable and fed him, then crept over to a hedge at the back of the house. People were out the front, talking. Two utes drove out along the road I had returned on, one with a spotlight on it. Shit, I thought, they're looking for me. There was no turning back then. I couldn't possibly walk out and say, 'Sorry, I was going to run away but changed my mind.' I crept into my room, which was an addition at the back of the house, packed my bag, and took off into the night. The farmhouse was not far out of town, and I knew the back streets well enough to get out onto the main highway without being seen. I ran most of the way, whenever I could without drawing attention to myself. And once I got past the town limits, I kept on running. I was very fit in those days.

I panicked whenever I saw car headlights approaching. I had to run a fair way into the bush to hide, for although there were plenty of trees along the highway, the undergrowth was sparse and I felt sure that all travelling eyes would be on me, that someone would drag me out and hand me over to the police. Then again, I had to be careful not to step into an old mine pit in the dark. Wedderburn was a gold mining town in the pioneer days, and the areas that were not being farmed were pitted with mounds and holes which were the remnants of diggings.

As it got late the traffic on the road ceased, apart from an occasional truck. I walked along the bitumen, enjoying the pale moonlight, the chilly air, the silence of the bush. My fear and anger melted away on that solitary walk; I felt calm and life was pleasant again. I was sure that everything had been that man's fault. I shut him out, shut the past out as though it had never existed. And I gave up worrying about the future; I knew I had no control over it, but was optimistic again that things would turn out right.

I don't know how far I walked that night. I got tired, my legs ached, and as the temperature dropped I began looking for somewhere to sleep. I pushed on a bit further, then saw a bridge ahead. There was a track leading down to a camping area, which I followed. Suddenly a dog started barking. It sounded very savage. I froze on the spot, my heart thumping. The barking stopped. When I moved forward, it started up again. The dog was obviously tied up, so I moved cautiously towards the noise until I could make out the shape of a truck, like a moving-van, near the trees at the edge of the clearing. I went up to the cab and tested the door. It wasn't locked, but the door hinge squeaked loudly which put the dog into a frenzy.

'Who's there?' came a rough voice from inside the back of the truck.

'It's me,' I said.

'Who are you?' I had to think for a while. I wasn't ready for questions. 'What do you want?' came the voice. That was easier. 'I'm looking for somewhere to sleep,' I yelled back.

'Okay. Get up in the cab.' Using my case for a pillow, I stretched out along the cab seats and went straight to sleep. I slept like the dead, my exhaustion catching up with me at last.

The sun was quite high when I woke up the next morning. I peered around outside, looking for the dog. It was a red heeler, and was over near the campfire next to an old man in grey overalls. He was cooking up a feed – and I was starving!

As I wandered over, the dog sat up. 'Sit down, Suzie,' said the old man in a familiar way. I could tell that these two had been together for a long time, that they had a bond. 'Come and have a feed,' he said to me, not taking his eyes off the job at hand. There was toast, grilled polony, tomato sauce, and a billy of tea. He divided the food equally then passed me a huge plateful. It was delicious, the best breakfast I could remember having. Polony fat and sauce dribbled down my hands and chin as I chewed, gulped and swallowed noisily. The old boy didn't seem to mind my lack of table manners, although I guessed he expected me to throw a bit of food to the dog every now and then, as he did. The dog was very well-mannered, sitting up straight, pretending to look uninterested, and gracefully catching each offering with only a slight snap of the teeth.

It was lovely down there by the river. There was a light breeze on my face, the sun on my back, and food in my belly. I was content; I wanted to stay there forever. We sat around drinking tea for quite a while, and although not pushy, he asked me where I'd come from and where I was going. I don't remember whether I told him lies, half-truths, or something else. I did lie about my age, for I knew that was a legal matter, me being a ward of the state. I think he guessed I was a runaway, but he offered me a job all the same.

'I'm a showie. I usually pick up a worker on the grounds at bigger shows, but you can be my offsider if you want. The pay won't be much, but you'll be fed and looked after as long as you're with me.'

I didn't answer straight away. I was wondering what would be involved in being an offsider. Did he want to screw me? I couldn't tell. Did old men screw? I didn't know the answer to that question either. I'd been screwed for as long as I could remember, by all sorts of men, but not by an old man. Still, I didn't see what difference it would make. Anyway, I thought, anything will be better than going back to Winlaton. I accepted his offer.

It was a great adventure for me, riding up front in a big truck, thinking of it as my new home. I had the same feeling I'd had in the train, of being carried along to new places, leaving behind old faces. In some ways it was better than the train. From the front of the truck I had a full view of the world, whereas in the train I'd only have a side view. And we could stop and start the truck whenever we wanted to; we weren't stuck to a timetable. Riding in the truck gave me a feeling of freedom, a new experience of freedom that I learnt to love. That freedom was an illusion, of course, but ignorance is often bliss when you are young.

We travelled up to Mildura, poking along at a steady speed, stopping here and there to clean up and eat. The showie took to calling me 'matey'. He enjoyed pointing out things of interest along the way, 'Hey matey, what do you think of that...?', and 'Hey matey, take a look at this...'

We got on very well together. He continued to use his bunk in the back for sleeping in, while I continued to camp in the cab. Suzie, the dog, travelled in a cage welded to the underneath of the truck. She was locked in there at night, but when he let her out in the mornings she would run about madly for a while, sniff around and do her business in the bush, then come back to the fire to oversee the cooking of breakfast.

Often the showie would burst into song while at the wheel. He sang happy songs such as 'Roll Out the Barrel,' and old nostalgic songs. He introduced me to the world of Nat King Cole, in particular to the song 'Stardust.' He sang it many times, whistling the tune where he couldn't remember the words, and I never got sick of listening to it. Some of the words evoked wonderful images in my mind: 'the nightingale/sings its fairytale', and I thought of 'stardust' as something real that had magical properties. Fairytales had been very real to me when I was little, and some aspects of them still remained part of my concept of reality during my teenage years. Magic appealed to me then. Today, nearly forty years later, I can still hear the old showie singing the words of that song: 'the melody/haunts my reverie…'

We worked a small show at Mildura, one day only. I helped with unpacking and assembling the stalls, which wasn't hard work. He had sideshow stalls, including clown's heads and a 'throw the hoops' stall, but no rides. The most exciting part for me initially was unpacking and setting out the prizes. It was like having access to a giant toy-box, a child's delight. But I soon learnt that the good prizes, the teddy-bears, dolls and puppet-monkeys, were not for giving away. They were the lure used to get people to play games of chance, and I was disappointed to find out that most games of chance are rigged or otherwise designed to exclude chance. The large toys were packed away again, ready to tempt more suckers at the next show. I asked the showie why people kept wasting money on these games. 'I don't twist their arms,' he said defensively. 'Anyway, sometimes a big prize goes off. I'm barely makin' expenses, you know.' I hadn't thought about expenses.

On the way out of Mildura we toured around, and stopped to buy a large bag of oranges from one of the orchard stalls. 'We'd better hoe into these,' said the showie, 'because we won't be able to take them across the border.' So, hoe into them we did. They were so sweet. We ate nearly half a bag of oranges that day. When we camped at night I had to rush off into the bush with excruciating stomach pains. I though I was going to die. Later than night I heard the old man calling out to me from the bunk. 'He-e-lp. Help me. Matey, come here and give us a hand, will you?' As soon as I climbed into the back of the truck I knew what was wrong. He'd shit his pants.

'Here, get rid of these,' he said, passing me his pyjama pants. 'And can you get us a bucket of water?' He looked very old, very sick, and very pathetic. I could hardly stand the smell, but I knew he needed my help because he was in too much pain to help himself. It took me a while, but I eventually got him cleaned up and comfortable. As I sat outside, still not feeling too well myself, I cursed those oranges. I realised I had never had to nurse anyone before. There was never any nursing done in our home. If Jack had a migraine, he had to suffer it alone. We children were not allowed to be sick, and if we made a bodily mess we had to clean it up ourselves. So nursing the old man was a new and slightly disturbing experience for me.

We drove down to Adelaide, then on to another small show on the coast somewhere. Then it was back to the big smoke for the Adelaide Royal Show. The showie took me to one of his favourite haunts in town for a special feed: steak, eggs, tomatoes and chips. It was good. Then he gave me some money – quite a lot – saying he wanted me to buy myself some new 'clobber and boots'.

I walked into town early the next morning, waiting for the shops to open. I didn't really know what I was looking for – until I saw the R.M. Williams shop. Wow, I thought, just what I need! There in the window, among saddles, hats, stock-whips and other exciting things, were several pairs of R.M. Williams's elastic-sided riding boots. I fell in love with them. But could I afford them? As soon as the store opened I went in and asked how much they were. I forget what the price was now, but they were going to cost me nearly all the money I had. Without hesitation, I bought them. I put them on, leaving my old and by then worn-out gumboots at the shop. I walked out on to the street feeling so proud. I kept looking at my reflection in any full-length windows I passed as I made my way back to the showgrounds.

When I got back to the truck, I lifted my feet to the old man, showing off my new leather boots. His face went blank. I guessed by his silence that I'd done something wrong, but I didn't know what. Later, he tried to explain to me, without hurting my feelings, that he'd wanted me to buy some 'decent' clothes. Shoes, not boots. I knew then I had disappointed him. As sex was not on the agenda, the only way I could make it up to him, I thought, was by working extra hard.

I did work hard at that show. They were long, tiring days and nights. I nearly yelled myself hoarse with 'Step up! Step up! Two bob a throw!' and various other calls I mimicked off the showies around me. I had a leather pouch around my waist which filled up rapidly with silver coins. Sometimes the old man took off for an hour or so, saying, 'Look after things, matey,' as he left. I was very pleased that he trusted me to look after things, and that he trusted me with the money. That was another new experience for me, being trusted. It was a new kind of freedom.

Towards the end of the show the old man told me he would be going back to Melbourne. He asked me to go with him, but didn't seem surprised when I said I'd rather not. I think he knew I was on the run, although I had nearly forgotten that fact myself, and he never mentioned it. I don't remember the day he left, or any farewells, but I know I was sad about our parting. He was a good friend.

CHAPTER 7

Revolving Doors

Recidivism

We are society's rubbish
recycled
again and again.

Greenough Regional Prison, 1994

N ow began, like a recurring bad dream, a traumatic cycle of imprisonment and escape, always running away and always giving myself up to those who would put me away again. Something in me was rebelling, but against what I didn't know. Worse, I was unable to see that running away was actually running towards the authorities and more punishment.

It began the day the showie and I said our goodbyes and I stayed on in Adelaide. By nightfall I was on the streets, this time with no money. Like a mouse in a maze I couldn't see a way out. Nan had drummed into me from an early age that I had to work for my keep, so asking for charity just didn't enter my mind. Unlike the mouse I didn't seek options but wandered aimlessly around suburban streets, walking here, sitting there, until it got late. I studied the somnolent, silent houses, knowing they had families inside, people cosy in their own beds, belonging, asleep and oblivious to me outside. I was lonely, an emotion I rarely felt. I thought of Jack and our old house in Doncaster; I wanted to go home.

In the early morning the police picked me up as I knew they would. I knew, too, they would send me back to Winlaton eventually, but I also knew I would be given a feed and bed for the night. They locked me in a single cell, kept me in isolation for two or three days, took me to court, then flew me back to Melbourne and drove me straight to Winlaton.

Obs Cell

canvas pyjama mattress
concrete bed
untearable quilt
plastic water-bottle
stainless-steel low-flush toilet
openless smashless windows
no power-points switches
protrusions or bars:
hang-proof cell
for the safety and observation
of suicidal prisoners
 after hours days and nights
of isolation cold and boredom

they come out promising
to be better

Greenough Regional Prison, 2 May 1993

Solitary confinement is supposed to subdue people. Time is supposed to wear them down. Back at Winlaton I spent many weeks in solitary but I didn't become grateful whenever a key turned in the door; I became hostile. I didn't become dependent on my keepers, waiting for them to bring me meals and a change of bed linen. Rather, they were an intrusion on my world of fantasy, which kept me occupied during most of my waking hours. Staring at a brick in the wall for hours on end mesmerised me, gave me a kind of inner peace.

My fantasies were always of far away, idyllic places, most of them remembered images from garish rural color photographs on low-grade paper. The *Australasian Post*, a magazine that featured buxom girls in bikinis beaming from the cover and dinki-di Aussie yarns, jokes and cartoons inside was my muse. One full-page photograph I dwelt on showed ultra-green hills, mauve mountains in the distance, a sapphire-blue river flowing gently in the foreground under overhanging river-gums, and a chestnut horse grazing contentedly on the hillside, its summer coat shining in the sun. In my fantasy I was in this scene, sitting on the river bank, not going anywhere or doing anything, just being, alive to the sounds of frogs, crickets and bird-calls, to the heat of the sun and the sharp coolness of the water, to the smells of summer grasses, damp earth and eucalyptus leaves – all the things I had loved as a child, things familiar and comforting. My fantasy scenes were all unpeopled. Alone in the bush I did not have to contend with the demands, criticisms and punishments of society, and I felt that was where I belonged. I

Brenda's mother Beryl Nanette MacKenzie (Nan) strikes a pose at Mickey Powell's Dance Studios, where she worked.

RIGHT: Brenda's stepfather Jack Mock on his racing bike.

BELOW: Brenda as a toddler with Bluey, the cocker spaniel, at Nanna Mock's.

BOTTOM: Jack and Brenda, as a teenager, in the kitchen at Doncaster, Victoria, with Pinny the cat.

Brenda's older brother Danny, his fiancee Linda and her younger brother Edd at Doncaster.

Danny and Edd before Danny's wedding in Frankston, Victoria.

Taken during the author's stint as camp cook at Milrose Station, Western Australia, where she worked for some geologists employed by Falconbridge mining company.

Sonia and Sandy, David Hodge's children, at the farm at Mt Helena, Western Australia. Brenda married Dave when she was 21 and he was 34.

Brenda in about 1977 with some of the dogs on the farm at Mt Helena – all strays that she'd taken in.

The new man in Brenda's life, Gordon, whom she met after her divorce while working at Jane Brook stud farm, in Stratton, Western Australia. He's pictured with their dog Boris

Gordon and Brenda relaxing at Lake Leschenaultia, Western Australia, in the 1980s.

The author at Jane Brook stud with two brumbies from Windida station. The grey mare on the right is Lucy, 'the best riding horse I ever had'.

Preparing yearlings at Jane Brook stud.

The manager of Jane Brook, Bill Ormsby, and Brenda taking youngsters out on a hunt. Brenda is on Moonshine, one of her show mares.

Brenda at Perth Royal Show with her other show mare Raindrop.

Brenda's only photo of herself at Greenough Prison, Female Block.

The other female prisoners at Greenough Prison, 1991.

Jenna, Brenda's friend in Boulder and Bandyup prisons – after her release.

Greenough Regional Prison. This photo was taken by the author as she stepped out into freedom in 1995. She planted the rose garden.

Banyup chaplain, Sister Marie O'Malley, 'being wonderfully informal' in her garden.

After Brenda's release, two of her most invaluable and consistent supporters, Father Brenton Taylor and Marlene Rousse, took her to Ellendale Pool for a picnic – and her first taste of the great outdoors in twelve years. Father Taylor and Brenda are pictured here.

Taken on the same day, Brenda savours the fresh air and sunshine at Ellendale Pool, near Geraldon, Western Australia.

Brenda's supervisor – and friend – Alison Dawson with chef Martin Padbury in St John of God Hospital kitchen, where she worked for nine years.

ABOVE AND BELOW: Janette, Brenda and Carole – the first meeting of the three sisters at Carlton, their birthplace, in 2003.

Some members of Janette's large family. Left to right: Naomi, Jimmy, Carole, Janette and Brenda.

Edd and Brenda at a surprise party her friends held for her in 2004.

ABOVE: Edd on holidays in Geraldton – with Jarrah.

RIGHT: Jarrah, 'my mate for the past ten years'.

was not troubled by life until keys opened the door and let in intruders.

One morning the door opened and I was told to get ready for a trip into town. Ten or twelve of us went in a departmental bus, supervised by Winlaton officers. We were taken to a large public hospital for another 'internal', an examination for venereal disease and pregnancy. I had already suffered one of these penetrating experiences on my re-admission, and I resented having to undergo another. There were two of us in the surgery with just one supervising officer when I saw a large pair of scissors on a tray by my hand. Out of character and on impulse I moved in front of the tray, took the scissors, and hid them in the pocket of my fully-flounced Winlaton skirt. We weren't searched either before leaving the hospital or on our return to Winlaton, and I was soon back in the cell with my prize. For a short time those scissors were my secret prized possession.

I had the idea of chipping the mortar away from a brick in the wall so I could slide it out whenever I wanted to talk to someone in the next cell. There was nothing to talk about really, but I wanted a secret to share with a friend. The cement was very hard, and I was absent-mindedly scratching at the wall one day when an officer burst into the cell. 'What are you doing!? What have you got there? Show me!' she screeched.

I ran at her with the scissors in my hand, trying to scream 'no' but unable to hear myself, feeling only the effort to say something, anything, in nothingness. I now know I had experienced another state of dissociation, a temporary split from reality and self which was the consequence of a prolonged period of stress and depression. My memory of the event contains only fragmented images. There is no memory of sound, emotion, or even tactile response; there was no feeling of having feet or hands, just a desperate struggle in the chest and throat to get something out of my mouth. Once the sense of self returned, which it did rapidly, the experience became a frightening one, for there was no longer any secure knowledge of who 'I' was.

The next thing I remember is being back in a cell, hiding in a corner from eyes and voices through the peephole. From down that end of the wing I could smell roast potatoes, Sunday lunch. 'I'm hungry!' I screamed, 'Hungry, hungry, hungry...' My stomach was in a knot, but finally I went silent. I had no more energy, emotional or physical. The police came and took me to a psychiatric hospital.

I was admitted to a ward at Larundel, a ward full of middle-aged and elderly people, all drugged continuously and at once I was given an elephantine-dose of Largactil. I slept for days. Coming out of those drug-induced time lapses was a bad experience. My head felt like lead. I didn't know where I was, and my legs and arms crumpled when I attempted to rise up from the bed, bench or floor where I had collapsed. There was a spinning sensation that took hours to stop, a mild nausea and/or sweating, an overwhelming sense of confusion, and a feeling that I was chained to the floor and might never stand or walk again. I now know I have an adverse reaction to tranquillizers. I didn't know that then. And neither did the people who were 'treating' me.

The drugs made me ravenous and in just a few months turned me from a normal teenager weighing around 54 kilograms to an obese 83 kilograms. Not that the food was good, or plentiful. The main meal of the day was often a slushy pale grey stew full of weevils. We had porridge in the mornings, always tasteless and never enough. I used to load mine with sugar, scoff it down, then look around for someone who had nodded off at the table so I could scoff theirs down too.

Nan visited me at Larundel. She proposed that we kill ourselves. We sat on a bench at the edge of the sports oval. She was in one of her serious, poetic moods. In her far-away voice she talked about 'this tired old world' and 'greener pastures in the beyond' – a metaphor she knew I would like. Then she said she wanted me to go with her.

'Just you and me together.' She looked at me. 'Well?'

'How would we do it?' I croaked.

'I can arrange it.' It occurred to me that she might arrange my death, but not her own. I began shaking, and then sniffling.

'I don't want to,' I choked. She erupted. 'You gutless little bitch! I knew I couldn't depend on you...'

She was still abusing me as I ran back to the ward, anywhere to get away from her. The nurses wanted to know what was wrong, but I didn't want to talk to them, and couldn't have even if I did want to. I couldn't stop crying, wailing loudly, gasping for breath and half choking on my tears. They gave me a large unscheduled dose of drugs, but after that wore off I was still deeply depressed. I couldn't shake it off. It was as though years of pain had come gushing up all at once.

Several days later I told one of the nurses what had happened. My mother was banned from visiting me and re-admitted to Royal Park Psychiatric.

Three times I ran away from Larundel. Once I'd started out just going for a walk through the hospital grounds, but I kept on going and I have no memory of what I did next or how I was returned to the hospital. The second time I remember vividly. Standing on a bench window in the dayroom one evening, I realised that the windows were only secured with a small block of wood and one nail. I was alone; everyone else was in bed or prepared for bed. I walked all the way to St Kilda beach, where, footsore and exhausted, I sheltered in a public lavatory. Someone with a heart saw me sitting in there and rang the police. They drove me back to Larundel.

I was feeling quite exuberant after my night out, but as soon as the police left and the door was shut behind me, I realised I was back in that 'other world' and tears started streaming down my face. The head nurse wanted me to take a large dose of Largactil. I pushed past her and ran screaming into the dayroom. Crying and screaming, I pummeled the windows and then I was being pulled down; men in white coats had my arms, my legs. I went down kicking and screaming. Three of them rolled me onto my stomach, pulled down my pants and jabbed a needle in my backside. It knocked me out. I came to the following afternoon in an observation room – solitary confinement. I was left there for nearly a week, and a doctor came to see me several times. 'How are you?' he always asked. It was impossible for me to explain how I was, so I always answered 'Good' just to please him. After he left, the charade over, I would cry. But the last time he visited me he came back to observe me through the peephole, caught me crying, and I caught him watching me. I hated him for that, and decided I wasn't going to talk to him anymore. But several days later I was taken to his office.

'We want you to take this,' he said. 'It's paraldehyde, nasty stuff I know, but it will be better for you if you swallow it down without any fuss. The injection is a very painful one.' I swallowed it down without any fuss, and was then taken over to Mont Park hospital, my new home.

Mont Park was in the same grounds as Larundel. There was no security fence, you could walk out from either – and I did – but while Larundel was a short-term psychiatric hospital Mont Park was a loony bin, a nut-house, the end of the road. The place of cages. People, caged during the day, paced around inside like animals in a zoo. Those lucky enough to have a tree in their cage walked around and around the tree, so that a trench was left around the base of the tree – a moat between the living dead and their keepers. I was kept in a two-storey red brick building with other women. We were only allowed out for twnety minutes a day under strict supervision.

Nan, just released from Royal Park, came to visit me again.

'When can I go home?' I asked her.

'Soon,' she kept saying but of course I didn't believe her. Three or four weeks after her last visit, when I was supposed to go to the section where trusted patients made pegs, I took off – my third escape – determined this time never to come back.

I hitchhiked out of Melbourne, up the Hume. Hitchhiking became a way of life for me, in between jobs, and I always felt safe with truckies. They were always on the move, like me, most of them detached from the norms of family and the social complexities of life, a detachment I could identify with. Life was 'Let's go', 'Let's eat', 'What about a quickie?', and 'Wake me up in two hours.' There was no excess baggage, emotional or material.

I was heading for Darwin, as far from Melbourne as possible, travelling light and fast. At the Threeways, a T-junction of the highways between Mt Isa, Darwin and Alice Springs, I was wandering around the service station while the truckie checked his tyres and ropes, when a green Mercedes pulled in. A big girl of about 22, blonde with long dark eyelashes, and in matador pants and high heels got out and wobbled over.

'G'day. How ya goin? Where you off to?'

'Darwin,' I said.

'Me too. You been before? You'll like it. It's big, but it's just a bloody country town, but everyone knows everyone and the weather's fantastic. Hot 'n' sexy. I love it.'

The driver, a bald, chain-smoking Italian, took no notice of me. The blonde was a chatterbox. She was Deborah from Mascot, Sydney, she told me, and when I asked her what she did for a living she said she was a 'worker'. She didn't look or sound like the prostitutes at Winlaton who 'worked' on the streets. Deborah was older, sophisticated, and she had a pimp.

'Whyncha come to Darwin with me and Chris? Do it in style. Meet some blokes, a few tinnies, have a lot of laughs.' She was so easy to talk to, and so bubbling over with plans about all the fun we'd have together. It sounded good to me and I told the truckie I was off with Deb and Chris in the Merc. He wasn't happy. He could see what I was heading into.

We stayed at a caravan park out of Darwin. Deborah – my pretend sister – and I never saw much of the pimp during the day, and we did have fun, but at night the pimp took us out. He and I sat in the car outside motels, hotels and houses while Deborah went to work. I asked her how she felt, doing it with strangers. 'Nothin'. I don't feel nothin',' she said, 'I just think about all that money.'

Then it was time I started thinking that way. We drove down to Tennant Creek, arrived at dusk, booked into a hotel for the night and went straight out to a mining camp. By now it was dark and all I could see were rows and rows of huts, 'dog-boxes', a jumble of lights that didn't seem to illuminate anything, and shadowy figures of men everywhere. Outside one long hut, milling in the dark, was a crowd of a couple of dozen, laughing coarsely, whistling, as big brassy Deborah in her tight T-shirt and short shorts and little me, in the same uniform, approached. They were clapping their hands, clutching their crotches, calling out in a babble of languages.

'Deb, I don't want to go in there,' I whispered in the quavering voice of the child I was. Deborah looked at me, a mix of exasperation and sympathy and, perhaps, a little sorrow. She shrugged: 'Bit late now, Bren.'

The pimp and Deborah went into one room and then it was my turn. He led me into a room empty except for a bunk with a white sheet in the middle of the room, and above it a large glaring light that gave the appearance of an operating theatre.

'Get your gear off and hop on,' the pimp said, patting the bunk. Then a miner came in. The two talked in what I took to be Italian and the pimp left. I lay there, waiting for the miner to 'do it'. He stood next to me naked, talking incomprehensibly, trying to show me what he wanted me to do to him. I didn't move, just stared at him, giving him my most stupid look. I'd lie there, but that was all I was obliged to do. He put his pants back on and stormed out. I heard them arguing outside, their voices raised and angry, then other voices joining in. It wasn't my inexperience that saved me that night, but my age. I was only fifteen. A lot of men like the idea of sex with minors but it's a crime, and child prostitution is particularly risky.

The pimp stuck his head round the door. 'We're getting out of here! Get dressed, shithead!'

We picked up Deborah, now frightened, and went back to town. They dropped me off outside the hotel and drove off with my belongings still in the car. No one said anything.

That left me stuck in a mining town with no money, and no clothes except the shorts and top I had on. I had to do something about my situation before it got much later. When life got too tough I had come to see the police as my protectors. I hung around the station until they eventually came outside and asked questions. I felt safe in the Tennant Creek lock-up, and was almost grateful when I was flown back to Melbourne.

I was sent back to Winlaton, but Winlaton didn't want me. In their opinion, I was mad, not bad. Then I was sent back to Mont Park but they didn't want me either. In their opinion, I wasn't mad enough. To complete the circle, I was sent back over to Larundel, but only because no one else would have me. According to records I was an embarrassment to the authorities, who didn't know what to do with me next. Larundel didn't want me either. I had emotional problems, not psychiatric ones.

Someone came up with the idea that I needed a family environment. 'Where is your real father? Would he take you?' They eventually contacted my biological father – probably through Nan.

It was a dream come true, then, when a nurse at Larundel told me that my biological father and his family in Queensland had agreed to take me. This time, I thought, things *will* turn out right. I had the idea that my father would look after me, protect me from all of life's obstacles and pain. More than that, though, I felt that at last I was being accepted by this man whose absence had given me a greater feeling of rejection than any of my mother's bitter words and long silences ever had.

CHAPTER 8

A 'Real' Father

I remember the nurses saying goodbye, telling me what a 'lucky girl' I was. I remember flying low over a river as the plane approached the Brisbane airport. And I remember my father, Harry Smith, coming out onto the tarmac to meet me, hugging me tightly. Then we went over to meet the family.

His wife Angela was a handsome woman, tall, elegant, with thick black hair. My half-sister, Pam, was a younger version of her mother. She was one year younger than me, but much more sophisticated and sure of herself. Then there was young Tony. He was four at the time. I was never able to think of him as my brother, or even as a relative. He stayed close to his mother most of the time, and the two of them remained strangers to me.

We drove home in the family station-wagon. It was a new car, and the house was neat and comfortable, a model Queenslander, built on stilts with deep verandahs and covered sleepouts. There were banana and mango trees, richly scented frangipanis and other exotic flowering shrubs and long lush grass which always needed mowing. The steamy humidity reminded me of Darwin. In the background was a chorus of cicadas and other insects clicking and whirring interminably. I thought I was in paradise.

It took me a while to get used to the habits of my new home. The first meal was especially strange. We all helped to prepare and cook it, mistakes were allowed, and my father wandered around the kitchen drinking wine. Fingers dived into the food bowls and pinched a bit as we went along. It was so different from the silent, military-style ritual my mother insisted upon.

I found a job in a fruit shop nearby. I had my unruly hair cut and shaped, bought some new clothes and soon had a boyfriend. He was nineteen, four years older than me. I had been 'dating' men in their twenties or thirties, with Nan's consent, since I was ten or eleven years old. This never involved much more than sex. Dating the boy from Brisbane was fun; we were involved with each other as people and that was something new for me. Then he joined the navy, to follow in his brother's footsteps and I never saw him again.

As for my father, a respectable man, running a successful business, he was an alcoholic. His wife kept the business going, and he could afford private treatment when he needed to dry out. Unlike Nan, who made a display of her drinking, my father could drink a lot of alcohol day and night and not show it – until he went on a bender. Then he had to go to hospital and he was 'out of town on business' to his customers. My father told me that he was an alcoholic. He also told me that my mother and the next-door neighbor at Wonga Park used to have sex while Jack was at work. He named the man, so I knew he must have got this information from my mother. Now I knew why I had been locked out of the house so often during my pre-school years. What I couldn't understand was why he was telling me about it.

My father took me out fairly often. One night, at a friend's home, posh people and all adults, I managed to get through dinner without making a fool of myself until one man decided to make sport of me. He sauntered over, eyed me off, then asked me about my Winlaton tattoos.

'What are they? A new kind of art form? Been living out in the desert with the Abos?' I burst into tears, ran out of the room to the main bedroom and threw myself on to the bed. My father followed and took me up in his arms to comfort me, holding me until I stopped crying. Then he laid me down on the bed and started rubbing against me. I had just been totally humiliated by one of his friends and he was getting horny! Abruptly he got off me and left the room. A few days later, in the middle of the afternoon, we were alone in the house. My father called from his room. 'Come here, I want you.' I had a good idea what he wanted, and I had no compunction about giving it to him. I was prepared to trade sex for love – what I thought was love. He started, him on top, me lying there and taking it. Suddenly he stopped and said, 'Can't you do anything!'

Do anything? What was I supposed to do? He spoke to me as though I was a whore, as though he wasn't getting his money's worth. I thought of Tennant Creek, of that night in the miner's hut. I thought of my mother, of what she might have been 'doing' at the moment of my conception. It was no good. I had given him all I had to give, and obviously that was not good enough. I felt ashamed of not being able to please my father, socially or sexually. I knew I was going to lose him again.

Life went on much the same after that day, except my father started drinking more heavily. His drinking became more obvious, and his wife made it clear she didn't want me there. Using the only coping strategy I had, I ran away.

I was back on the streets, in a city I didn't know. Not that there was much difference – all cities are cold and impersonal when you are walking the streets on your own. I wasn't destitute. I could have rung my father at any time and he would come to get me. But I would have had to live by his terms, pretend that he wasn't abusing me, pretend I was part of the family when I felt strongly that I wasn't. The police duly picked me up and took me down to the station. I spent what was left of the night in the lock-up.

My day in court was unusual in that it took a long time for any decision to be made about what to do with me. Although I didn't know it at the time, I was what is known as a 'status offender' that is, I was 'guilty' of 'offences so designated because of the offender's status as a juvenile... In the majority of cases it appears that sexual behaviour perceived as inappropriate prompted the Children's Court to make an order for care and control' (*Forde Closed Report*, Karrala, page 3). My father was there, even though he was a participant of my 'inappropriate sexual behaviour'. He alone spoke to the judge. The police kept on giving me odd looks, but didn't speak to me at all. Other people were called in and out, private discussions stopped and started, started and stopped. Everyone was talking *about* me, but not *to* me.

People always treated me differently once they knew I had been in a psychiatric hospital. They stood further away from me, whispered among themselves, watched me furtively as though too much eye contact might somehow contaminate them. The stigma of having been in a psychiatric hospital is one that separates and excludes, that results in the labeled person being 'put away' again and again, often into hellish places. The Brisbane court sent me to one such place, a place called Sandy Gallop.

Sandy Gallop was like no other institution I have ever been in. I didn't know what sort of institution it was. There was another building, further up the hill, which must have been for women. One woman, who sounded quite old, used to scream and wail bitterly every night.

I never saw or heard any other girls in my section. The only people I had contact with the whole time I was there were five warders who were dressed all in white, one matron, and one male doctor. I was locked in a fairly large room with a metal bed in it, and there was a window which I stared out for hours at a time, but never saw anyone. There were no gardens. The place was nothing more than a large, dry paddock with a wire security fence around it. A few dirt tracks connected the drab, isolated, buildings inside the compound.

Once every two or three days, the mango man, in an old white ute, came hurtling down the hill in a cloud of dust. He bought turpentine mangoes – excess fruit or seconds – for the inmates, patients, or whatever we were. Watching their arrival, then eating them, were the only pleasant experiences I had in that place.

The women warders who worked at Sandy Gallop were different from those at Winlaton. They had no pretence of being human. They only ever spoke to give an order, usually to take medication and to go for a shower. The two went hand in hand; I would take the medication, then when it started to take effect they would help me to the shower – that is, prop me up like an old drunk, because my legs wouldn't carry me and I couldn't keep my balance. I don't know what sort of medication it was, but it was quick-acting and powerful. No one spoke to me through the showering procedure. When it was finished I was dressed, taken back to my room, and locked in without books or writing paper, just left with nothing to do but wait for the next meal. Meal times were my markers of time. They gave me the assurance that time was passing, the world was still turning.

A strange thing happened after I'd been in that room for a few weeks. I started making milk, or at least, a fluid started seeping from my right breast. It was enough to leave wet patches on my shirt. I can only presume now that it was a result of the heavy medication they were forcing me to take. I also began fainting at odd times. On one occasion I came out of the faint flat on my back on the bare wooden floor, surrounded by the legs of the matron and her cohorts. They were standing around me in a half circle, staring down at me in stern silence. The matron pronounced: 'This girl needs more exercise.' More exercise? Any exercise would be an improvement.

I was also having crying fits. The medication seemed to induce depression when it was wearing off, although my lack of normal activity might have been a contributing factor. Sometimes when the woman up the hill screamed, I screamed too. Screaming for no apparent reason is a way of venting pent-up emotions, is a way of saying what can't be said in a world void of communication. Her screaming frightened me a little because I couldn't see her, couldn't put a face to her, but she was an echo of my unreal cut-off self.

When I got too noisy they put me in a dark cell. It was the same size room, but had nothing in it other than a canvas blanket. The window was completely covered with heavy wooden shutters, and the light – controlled from outside the door – was not turned on for days at a time. Large cockroaches crawled around the room, and over me while I slept. The thought of them kept me almost paralysed with fright during my first days and nights in the dark cell.

I didn't get any mangoes while I was on punishment. I was fed on a plastic plate, and the light was left on while I ate. As soon as I had finished eating, the plastic plate would be whisked away and the light turned off again. I became badly constipated. For ten days I kept eating but passed nothing. The pain was terrible, and I felt sure I was left in that state in accordance with the archaic belief that suffering purges the soul. However, it wasn't my soul that needed purging. Eventually, when I became doubled up with pain, they gave me something to clean me out.

A doctor came to see me twice. I wouldn't talk to him the first time. He came back the next day, turned the light on, and gave me some chalk. There was a blackboard on one of the walls, and he wanted me to spend an hour or so drawing whatever I liked. I knew from past experience he was going to make some meaning out of my drawings, so I drew a horse and a cross. To me, this was an expression of my grief, my loss of freedom. However, when he came back to see my drawings, all he did was give me a lecture on wild horses, on how they had to be 'broken in', 'tamed' or else 'put down'. I was amazed. I knew animals were put down; my pony had been put down. But I didn't know that people were put down too, which was what he seemed to be implying would happen to me if I didn't stop being 'wild'.

A few days later they put me back in the room with the window and lots of light. Being let out of near continual darkness was like being let out of a coffin. But as the silence and isolation continued, I felt no joy. It was almost as though too much emotional pain had deadened my senses. Not long after, I saw an eye peering at me though the peephole. I 'lost it', cracked up, went berserk. I lifted my bed right off the floor and hurled it against the wall. The ends fell off it. I grabbed one of the ends and ran to the peephole, smashed at it with a leg off the bed-end with such force that it shattered the plate-glass and went right through. I left the bed-end hanging in the door, then turned on the rest of the pieces which I hurled with fury all over the room. I was screaming again, shouting obscenities, smashing and throwing and ripping what I could, banging my head on the wall, kicking and pummeling the door. Eventually I wore myself out. This was not a dissociative experience, for I was aware of who I was and what I was doing. It was pure rage, one which a psychiatrist has since told me was a case of 'justifiable rage'.

No one came near me for the rest of the day, and I got no tea that night. The next morning the police arrived. I was heavily sedated, put in the police van, then – after six or seven weeks of sheer hell – was taken to Goodna Mental Hospital.

A sprawling establishment set in parkland gardens over an area nearly the size of a suburb, Goodna was a collection of various sections separated by large patches of bushland and connected with new bitumen roads. Some of the buildings were made of wood, some were red brick monstrosities. All the buildings down our end were old, mildewed and infested with cockroaches. I didn't see much of the place for the first few months; I was kept in a locked ward. There our only exercise was folding laundry out on an enclosed verandah, five days a week. I never saw anyone have a visit on the weekend, and I never had any visits myself. The food was worse, much worse, than the food at Larundel. The ward was dark and cramped. And, as usual, medication was compulsory so that most of the time we were all kept zombified. I was back in the land of the living dead.

The worst thing about being in that locked ward for me was waiting, waiting, waiting, waiting. From inside the trellised verandah I could hear traffic moving along the highway in the distance. I yearned for the day when I would be out on that highway, leaving this new nightmare behind. But I had no idea when that might be. Once inside a mental hospital it is hard to get out. People in such places are not only 'put away', they are also largely forgotten by friends, relatives, and the rest of the world. They are deemed to be no longer useful to society.

As I was folding laundry one day, a tear just popped out and dropped down one cheek and then I started to cry. I hadn't cried for a long time, and in a way I was pleased that I could still do it. Crying was part of my real self, my undrugged self, which I rediscovered on that day. The sister came over and shepherded me away from the other women.

'Are you getting upset, dear? Would you like to spend some time on your own?' I said I would. They took me down to an antiquated padded cell with a huge metal door on it. It looked like a vault in a medieval castle. Before I knew it I was trussed in a straightjacket, rolled onto my stomach, and given a needle in the bum. I didn't fight the needle that time (you can't fight anything in a straightjacket), but like the last jab I'd had in the bum it was very painful. I made a point of not crying in front of anyone after that.

Like all other institutions I had been in, Goodna seemed as much concerned with probing the body as it was with controlling the mind. After a few weeks I had to go with all the other recent admissions to be internally examined. But first we had to have an enema. I tried to object to this deeply humiliating practice although I knew I could not simply refuse it. As with all things in my life, if I didn't submit I would be forced. My feelings and fears were not taken into account; everything was said to be done 'for your own good'. I hated that feeling of being totally defenseless, of being powerless to stop people doing whatever they liked to me.

The wards at Goodna varied from locked to semi-open to fully open and the patients had to graduate through these wards before becoming eligible for release. Many, of course, were never released. While the rest of us were in a long dormitory there was one, a very old woman, who lived in a single room – in other words she existed on the bed day in and day out. She was fed, washed and toileted there. She was in the habit of tearing her clothes off, lying on her back, and kicking in the air with legs and arms – as a baby does before it is old enough to sit up on his own. She was doing that when I first saw her, thrashing with legs and arms, exposing all her private parts, and pulling weird faces. I tried to talk to her, but she didn't acknowledge me. I asked one of the nurses about this woman and she advised me not to go near her – she could become violent. (Many nurses and doctors were violent to patients; but controlled violence is sanctioned.) Another nurse told me the old woman was very rich, and that her relatives had put her in Goodna so they could get her money and that she had deteriorated rapidly since they'd had her committed. I saw her again about a month later. She was being wheeled down the road in a covered trolley to the hospital mortuary.

Many of the women in the semi-open ward were given ECT, electro-convulsive therapy – shock therapy. On the morning of treatment they milled around, terrified or excited or both; generating a quiet frenzy that affected others in the ward who never knew when their name might be added to the list. I lived in terror of ECT. I watched the women before and after treatment, and knew I did not want to share their experience. They came out of it greatly subdued and confused. Some of them could not remember their name for two or three days after and it was as though each one's self had been sucked out and only the shell of a person remained.

Eventually I was sent to an open ward. Winter was nearly over, and life in the open ward was not too bad. We all had to help clean the dayroom and dining room after breakfast, then had the rest of the day to wander around outside. As with Larundel and Mont Park, there was no security fence around the perimeter. I thought of running several times, but knew that if I wanted to stay out I would have to be released with papers. I did not want to go back to the locked wards.

My father came to see me one day. His visit was unexpected. I was sitting under a tree across the road from my ward when he drove up. He stepped out of the car, then just stood there, looking at me. My interpretation of that look was that he loved me, his daughter, yet was also ashamed of me, his daughter in the nut-house. I couldn't think of anything to say. He walked over and talked to me for a few minutes (I can't remember about what), then handed me a carton of Marlboros and left. I felt he had done me a kindness by visiting me, that I was not worthy of his time and concern. Old emotions had been stirred up, and I cried as he drove away.

Towards the end of my time at Goodna, I was sent to see a psychiatrist. Instead of asking me how I was getting on (the standard question), he read out bits and pieces from a stack of reports he had on me. They were mostly favourable. Then he told me it was time I started thinking about my future. But by that stage I didn't really want to leave the hospital. 'I've got nowhere to go,' I said. He said he would make some enquiries.

A woman came out to see me about a week later. 'Hi, I'm Rita, Rita Malone.' Rita Malone was buoyant, with a bouncing step and a huge Bugs Bunny smile. She never walked – she strode out head forward, like a kid setting out on a hike. She was full of business, full of life, and full of goodwill. I was cautious with her at first. I didn't know what authority she had, or where she was going to take me. But Rita wasn't into laying down the law. She asked me a few questions about my family's whereabouts, then asked me where I had come from before being sent to Goodna.

'Sandy Gallop,' I said.

'That place!' she hissed through her large white teeth. 'We've been trying to get that placed closed down for the past two years. Five girls have suicided out there...' Her voice got louder and her face got redder as she expounded on the atrocities of Sandy Gallop. I couldn't help smiling. I knew then that she was a friend.

Rita wasn't a person to beat around the bush. Did I have any money? Did I have any clothes? Did I want my tattoos removed? The last question stunned me. I desperately wanted my tattoos removed, but hadn't thought it would be possible. I told Rita I was very embarrassed about the tattoos, and she convinced the authorities to send me to a general hospital to get them surgically removed. I can laugh about it now, imagining her in the chief administrator's office, thumping her fist on his table and insisting, it is IM-PER-A-TIVE those tattoos come off! She was a very determined and persuasive woman.

Some weeks after I returned from the general hospital, I was released into Rita's care. She arrived to pick me up in her yellow Hillman. She bounced out, put her hands on her hips, and beamed a huge smile at me. Her face was all teeth and sunglasses. She was wearing a red cotton top, black stretch slacks and leather sandals. 'Well?' she asked through that wide grin of hers. 'You ready to go?'

CHAPTER 9

Sixteen

The house was a large old Queenslander, bigger than my father's, but run down. It was a women's refuge, run by Rita and Eilleen. Eilleen was an older woman who had entered the convent years ago and left before taking her final vows. She organised the household, the cooking, shopping, washing, lawn-mowing and all other routine jobs around the place. Rita had an outside job as a radio operator for a taxi company. She usually worked the afternoon/night shift, then spent the early mornings doing voluntary work with street kids, mainly young girls.

Rita told me she was a top radio operator, and I had no doubt it was true. She wouldn't have been a good taxi driver though. Rita was heavy-footed, always in a hurry. She always had too much to do. Her stamina amazed me. After working all night and well into the morning, she would come home for a few hours' sleep, then through the heat of the day go on charity drives, take sick kids to hospital, fix the decrepit plumbing, or paint the kitchen bright yellow. There was a sense of urgency about everything she did, but never a sense of burden.

There was never any extra food at the refuge. The women who had an income bought their own fruit and biscuits. The rest of us went without. We had cereal for breakfast, sandwiches for lunch, and stew or broth for tea. If extra women and children arrived at tea time, Eilleen would look up to heaven then scrape some stew off our plates onto however many more plates were needed, dividing the food as equally as she could. Watching her divide the food had a strong impact on me. It was the first time I had seen generosity displayed when there was so little to be generous with. Eilleen's selflessness and dedication to other people struck me deeply, and although I had rejected God, I couldn't help feeling that Eilleen and Rita were his angels at work – the guardian angels of women and children who were destitute or running scared.

Eilleen spent a lot of time in prayer. She carried her beads at all times, saying the rosary over and over when things were looking desperate. Finances were always desperate, but somehow we managed from day to day. I decided I should start bringing some money in, but I wasn't game to apply for a regular job. If employers found out I had been in Goodna, I thought, I'd be laughed at and rejected. I went door-knocking instead.

It was uncomfortably humid as I trudged around Brisbane's hilly suburbs looking for odd jobs. Some of the householders looked at me with distrust at first, but when I told them I was from the women's refuge most were happy to give me an hour or two of work cleaning windows, vacuuming, tidying up the garden or something similar. I began to feel useful again.

Sometimes I went with Rita on her charity drives. It wasn't what you would call fun, but it wasn't boring either. We visited private homes, libraries, the convent, old people's homes, and Rita would run in and out, delivering, exchanging, or collecting needed items.

She was so fast she was like a milko doing his early morning rounds, but she still made time to chat with everyone she met, always with that wide smile of hers flashing. We collected books for the old people, and the old people in turn made things for our annual fete.

The refuge gave only temporary accommodation for those in need. Rita arranged for me to move into a flat with a woman named Lorraine and a pregnant girl, Sandra, to make more room at the refuge and to get me started on a more independent lifestyle. The flat was close to the city, upstairs in a shabby old building. The three of us got on well, but I felt as though I was back in a hospital ward. I spent much of my time staring out a window, as there was nothing else to do. Sandra spent a lot of time sleeping, or crying because her parents and boyfriend had disowned her. And Lorraine had a busy social life dating men when not at work. As usual, I sat around waiting for someone else to make my life interesting. Having turned a blind eye to my real problems, I began worrying about being overweight. I bought appetite-suppressing diet pills containing amphetamines. By the end of the week I had lost control. I stopped eating. I had an insatiable need for coffee. I couldn't keep still for five minutes, pacing the room even while I was drinking the coffee. And my mind would 'take off' so that I didn't hear most of what anyone said to me. Sometimes I felt as though things were bombarding me. I lost track of time and reality.

One night I ran out of the flat, my mind frantic. I ran and ran barefoot through the streets as though a wild wind had picked me up and was carrying me, lifting me, pushing me on and on and on. I couldn't stop. I felt as though I had unlimited energy. The next thing I remember is lying face down and spread-eagled in the middle of a road just below a crest. I thought a car might come over the hill and squash me. I looked up, waiting for the lights, but nothing happened.

My next memory is of being down at the city lock-up, still spaced out, but no longer on the move. I rang Rita the next morning. She told me not to move, that she was coming up from Stradbroke Island to get me.

Speeding down the coastal highway in Rita's yellow Hillman was wonderful. I didn't know how far we were going, or for how long, but I was glad to be leaving Brisbane behind. Rita was back to her jolly old self, and it was a beautiful day. The air seemed to be fresher once we got out of the city. The sun was hot; but the world beyond the city seemed crisper, the colours brighter. I felt as though we were travelling into the dreamland of a glossy travel brochure.

We crossed from the mainland to the island over a narrow wooden bridge and drove on to a narrow pot-holed strip of bitumen that wound through dry bush to the far end of the island where there was a settlement: a post office, a shop, and about twenty houses, beach cottages or shacks depending on who owned them. Rita's friend Verna owned one of them.

Verna was a mystery. Her husband had disappeared in mangrove country up on the far north coast and after seven years had been declared dead. With the money from the estate she'd bought the little place on South Stradbroke.

Rita went straight back to Brisbane to help Eileen sort things out at the refuge. I settled into a peaceful life on the island. I stayed with Verna for nearly six weeks. I didn't think about my past or my future while I was there, I just enjoyed it day by day. I knew it would not last forever though. Rita rang one day to tell me she was coming down to get me.

A few days later, Rita and I were standing at the bus terminal in Brisbane. I was going to Rockhampton. A married couple she knew would pick me up at the other end, take me in for a while, and help me find a job. I thought it was a temporary arrangement but just before I boarded the bus Rita said to me, 'You're sixteen now. You're not a child anymore, you have to start looking after yourself.' I was shocked. She had never spoken to me like that before. My first reaction was to feel deeply hurt. I thought she wanted to get rid of me, that I must have been too much trouble and she was sick of me. However, at the same time another voice in the back of mind broke through the emotion, saying, 'She's right, you've got to learn to look after yourself.'

It was a turning point in my life. For the first time I realised that I too could make decisions and that I had to start making the right ones if I was ever to get off the merry-go-round of police, lock-ups and institutions. I thought about these things during the long bus trip up the coast, and although I was heading into the unknown, I felt good about making a fresh start.

Rita's friends in Rockhampton were in their mid thirties, a professional couple. I was uncomfortable in the house, afraid I might accidentally break something, and I felt like an intruder on their orderly domain. However, there I was, and we all made the best of it. The woman was very kind to me, taking me to interviews for jobs and trying to keep me company without being intrusive or patronising. We had nothing in common, but I knew she was doing her best to help me get a new start.

Eventually a job came up for a housekeeper/nanny. I started work with a young couple who had a gorgeous three-year-old son. He had thick golden-red hair and a quiet disposition. They were living in their townhouse at the time because Susan was pregnant and needed to stay close to the hospital. They also had a large cattle property west of the ranges, and when she later lost the baby we shifted out there for a while. It was a nice place. I went mustering once and that was fun. But after a few months we shifted back into town. There was tension in the family, and I wasn't happy in that situation anymore so I packed my few things – once again – and left.

I went home to my father. I was a different person now, and hoped that he might be different too. We could start again, pretend nothing had happened. When I arrived back at my father's house, I was stunned to find Lorraine there. How she came to know my father, I don't know. But I knew straight away she was having an affair with him. She avoided looking directly at me as she claimed she was his secretary. I told her I was going to ask him if I could be part of the family again.

My father and his wife and son were away in Sydney for a week, so there was just Pam, Lorraine and me in the house. We lay around eating snacks and playing board games until the day before they were due back, when we got stuck into the housework, did all the washing, and mowed the lawn.

I thought my father would be happy to see me again, but he didn't show it. His wife was definitely not happy about me being there. She had a violent argument with my father that she ended by yelling: 'If you don't get that little slut out of this house, I'm leaving with Tony and we won't be back!'

He came to me and said, 'Brenda. I'm sorry. I really am. But you'll have to go.'

Something inside me died. I couldn't speak. I packed my bag and walked out of the house, silent tears running down my face. Lorraine ran after me. 'Hang on,' she called out. 'You can stay at my place. I'm going there now. Get in the car... come on!' I sat in the car, waiting for her to get her things. The tears wouldn't stop. I felt as though I was turning into stone, with all my old self pouring out of my eyes. Soon I would be a dry, hard rock. Soon I will be empty of tears, I thought, and there will be nothing of me left, no pain, nothing.

Lorraine had a new flat, a ground-floor flat with a neat and pleasant little garden, not far from my father's. He had obviously set her up there, and I wasn't surprised by that. I didn't care about her, only about my father. I just couldn't believe he would throw me out, but he had. How could he do this to me? I was so hurt by his decision that I couldn't see he really didn't have any choice. I couldn't see he would lose his wife and only son; I could only see that he had thrown me out, didn't want me, wanted to get rid of me. I was back under the house at Doncaster, hearing my brother's words: 'Your father lives in Melbourne, and Mum goes to see him…'

Later that night he drove up at the back of the flat. Lorraine went out and spoke to him, then came inside and told me he wanted to talk to me. 'No!' The big 'no' that had been wanting to come out for years finally made its way out of my mouth. I knew then I had crossed over a line and would never go back. I had separated myself from my father, rejected forever that man who had twice rejected me.

Lorraine went out and told him, then came back and tried again. 'He cares about you, and just wants to talk to you for a few minutes,' she said. 'He wants to give you some money to help you out.' I told her to tell him what to do with his money, then went to bed.

The next day I went to the employment office and got a job as a barmaid in a pub at Goondiwindi. I told them I was eighteen and that I would work for board and keep until I learnt the job. I bought a bus ticket, and early next morning was heading west on a Greyhound coach. There had been some heavy rain overnight; creeks were running, gum trees were shimmering, and deep pools of water sheeted the sides of the road. The window between me and the world was slightly fogged, but it let in the light and kept out the cold.

CHAPTER 10

A Rolling Stone

My job as a barmaid at Goondiwindi lasted a week. I hated it – the smell of the bar, the groping drunks, the noise, the smoke; it reminded me of earlier days with my mother in Melbourne pubs.

As soon as I got my first pay packet I hitched with a truckie back to Brisbane and jumped a train to Townsville, travelling in the baggage compartment with two boys and leaping out and scrambling off, laughing with glee, as the train slowed to pull into the station.

I hitched with the boys over to Mt Isa, a rough mining town then and no place for a teenage girl. But I had my independence: no mother, no police, no jailers, no doctors. I was alone, happily sitting in a Mt Isa cafe, a short tousled-haired blonde in a T-shirt, jeans and sand shoes. From the jukebox Burl Ives was crooning *Pearly Shells* and I sang along, legs swinging as I sipped a Blue Heaven milkshake.

> ...*Pearly shells,*
> *from the ocean,*

shining in the sun,
covering the shore....

So there I was and from now on it seemed to me there was going to be plenty of pearly shells on my imaginary seashore.

I was half right.

There was a job going at Barry Caves, a motel roadhouse in the Northern Territory. They wanted an all-rounder – someone to help the cook, serve petrol and sell grog. I was hired by Barry Caves's owner, an old boy called Peg-Leg Fred, because he had a wooden stump which he'd swing from the hip with great dexterity. He worked hard, but he drank hard. Then, his wife Barbara would dump him in a wheelbarrow, take his leg off, and put him to bed. Sometimes Peg-Leg would come to, bounce back on hands and buttocks over the red gravel to the bar, hoist himself up on to a corner bar stool and order more drinks. We all had a good laugh with Fred.

Fred had a mechanic, Paddy, a full-blood Aboriginal who knew all about how to pull an engine apart but not much about how to put it together again. Fred was teaching him the job. Slowly. As far as Fred was concerned the longer he had to wait for parts, and the longer they took to put in, the more the tourists had to spend on accommodation. They didn't have much choice with their vehicle pulled to pieces; some were stuck at the Caves for weeks.

The bar work at Barry Caves was fine. Beer was only in bottles, and most of the customers were tourists and truckies, on the move and not interested in heavy drinking sessions. The bar was small and horseshoe shaped; there was a piano over to one side.

When two young Kiwis came in one night, one went straight to the piano and started playing a boogie number. The other, John, a redhead, sat at the bar and made friends with everyone. The Kiwis

109

were telecommunications workers, booked into the motel for a week. In that week I fell for John and he took a shine to me. We'd drive out into the desert, get out of the car and lie on a rug together, looking up at the vast darkness of Northern Territory's night sky and its awesome stars. The stars burn brighter there than anywhere else. Anyone who has travelled up that way knows I'm right. You can watch the Territory night-sky for hours.

We were in love, so I thought. And then I lost him – temporarily.

It was a particularly hectic time. Barbara was away, Fred was legless in more ways than one, the cook had also retreated to the inside of a bottle, and John and I and the barmaid Esmé were running the place. We had to stay open all night it was so busy, and after working all day I was exhausted.

With a long night ahead, one of the truckies offered me some of his No-Doze tablets. I thought, 'OK. But only until Barbara comes back.' I took one, and was soon wide awake. No-Doze was a bit like the diet tablets I'd taken in Brisbane and I was soon taking more and more of them. I went hyper, and then loopy. As the dawn was breaking, I took all my belongings to the incinerator out back – clothes, photos, everything – and burnt the lot. My head was spinning, but I knew what I was doing. I just don't know why I did it.

I started seeing things coming at me. I developed a severe and uncontrolled blinking and ducking behaviour. I had to get away. I cadged a ride in a cattle truck to the Threeways near Tennant Creek, and from there I don't know where we went because I passed out. I could have been in that truck for twenty-four hours or four days. The driver was worried when he dropped me off in Alice Springs. 'Get yourself to the hospital, love,' he said, but instead I walked down to the Todd River and crashed in the dry riverbed.

When I came to I walked the streets of Alice Springs looking for work. I got two weeks' work at a garage, cleaning out the long pits used to service buses. I was living on Salada crackers and sardines when I literally bumped into John at the supermarket.

As I turned around the aisle, my frugal trolley collided with another. It seemed overflowing with steak, eggs, bread and fruit – bushy blokes' food – and it was steered by a tall ginger-haired man with an endearing smile that I knew and loved. John had come to the Alice and got a job as a mechanic – his old trade – at another garage. He'd bought a caravan and we were soon living together in a caravan park at 'the Gap'. Hundreds of squabbling galahs woke us in the mornings, and as the sun came up we'd sit outside the van with a cup of tea, watching the rocky Gorge change colour every few seconds. We were happy then.

But I didn't take the Pill (I never had) and I didn't get pregnant. John wanted to get married and start his own family and my apparent sterility and bouts of depression led him to start looking around. He was never unfaithful but I decided to leave him before he kicked me out – another destructive life script that I had no awareness of until it was too late.

It was a sad parting. John must have given me some money to fly back to Melbourne, and I ended up back at Doncaster, at Jack's place, my old home. When I was depressed I always wanted to go home, but when I got there it wasn't any good. I didn't even know the word 'depression', much less have an understanding of it. I just thought if I went somewhere else it would go away. Sometimes it did, most times it didn't.

After a few days of moping around, missing John, hating the cold weather and life in general, I went to the races to see if I could find any of my old horsey friends. I knew one of the blacksmiths, a good-looking, well-muscled hunk, dark with curly hair, in his early twenties. He seemed to like everybody – even me – so I was thrilled when he asked me out to a dinner party at a friend's place in Surrey Hills.

When we got there, he just dumped me – introduced me to a few people then left me. I was incapable of mingling, making small talk with strangers, and I looked around the house for somewhere to lie down. I went into one of the bedrooms. An almost overpowering smell of stale urine hit me. I turned the light on. A tiny girl, five or six years old, paper thin, was lying on her back in a large, reeking cot... silent, staring at the roof, oblivious. It was cold, but she had on only a thin cotton nightie. I ran back into the party and found my date.

'There's a girl in there, in the bedroom. She's cold!'

'Mind your own business!'

'But there's something wrong with her... She can't speak... Who is she?'

'Stay out of it!'

'But why... what's wrong with her...?'

He grabbed me by the arm and bundled me into the kitchen. 'The kid's slow.' He was exasperated. 'She'll never be any good. The neighbours have already rung the Welfare twice, and my friends aren't too happy about interfering busy-bodies. Leave it alone! Get it!'

I felt guilty. Guilty because I was too scared to do anything or say anymore about the child in the cot. I went into the main bedroom, curled up on top of the bed and went to sleep. I oversleep when I'm depressed and on that night I went into a deep sleep.

Suddenly, the lights were on and my friend was standing over me, naked from the waist down. There was no romance, of course, just hard and fast sex. I was glad to get it over with.

'When are we going?' I asked.

'Not for a while. My mate wants a go with you?' His voice trailed off as in a question.

'No, I don't want to. I want to go home.'

'Well, tough!' Nasty now. He jumped off the bed, put his pants on and left. A few minutes later he was back, with his mate. He had a rifle. He pointed it at me. 'This thing's loaded. Are you gonna give my mate a go now?'

'No!' I said, surprising even myself.

BANG! He fired a shot into the wall within arm's length from my head. So his mate screwed me, and they both left. It wasn't until I got outside and started running that I realised how terrified I was. What if they followed me? They might shoot me to shut me up!

But no one followed me. They thought I was a joke, a 'bit of fluff' – that's all. I eventually found a phone box, hoping there would be a free taxi number: There wasn't. I sat on the floor of the phone box, shaking, and sobbing uncontrollably. It didn't occur to me, later, to report the rape. It wasn't part of our 'culture' in those days. Young girls out on the streets at night deserved to be raped, so it seemed.

Within months I was back in Alice looking for John. He was working at a mine. I rang him but he said he didn't want me to come back. He wasn't bitter, or deliberately hurtful. But I was devastated. I felt I'd come to the end of the line. I booked into a motel and took an overdose. It isn't easy with a bottle of tablets – it has to be done slowly so you don't gag and throw up. I got most of them down before I passed out.

I slept for two or three days. Then one of the motel cleaners, a young girl with olive skin, and dark hair pulled back in a pony-tail, found me. 'Excuse me. Are you alright?' She was a blur. I remember seeing her, trying to get up off the bed, then passing out again. She came back in the afternoon to see how I was.

'I've taken away the rest of your tablets,' she said – half statement, half query for permission.

'I did this once,' she said. 'It's not worth it, really. Whatever's happened, you're better off to forget it and make a new start.'

Her advice wasn't outstanding or awe-inspiring. It was the fact that she cared about me, that she hadn't rung the police and had me committed, and the fact that she had made arrangements for me to catch a bus to Darwin, meet with a friend of hers and get a job. I never knew her name, never saw her again, but I will never forget that girl who did more for me than so many 'servants of the state' have ever done. She was one of those wonderful people in my life who helped me to help myself.

I was ill on the bus trip to Darwin, too ill to sit up. I met the girl I was supposed to. She lived and worked at a pub in Darwin. She gave me enough money for a week's accommodation and a new set of clothes. 'Pay it back when you can,' she said. 'I'm not worried about it.' She also told me where to go to look for work. I didn't want to work in a pub so I applied for a job in the canteen of Rum Jungle, a uranium mine south of Darwin.

I was interviewed by an Army man who drove me down there the next day, stopping on the way to show me the famous 'magnetic anthills', and a large lake just off the main road, full of waterbirds, ibis, herons, storks – the Jabiru – and thousands of smaller birds. We drove up to the edge of the water and they took to the air – a white cloud simultaneously billowing up into the sky, then settling again like snowflakes at the far edge of the lake. At Rum Jungle I was introduced to people I would be working with, shown the canteen and dropped off at the female quarters. Rum Jungle looked great: not too big or small, not too noisy, and the people I was to work with seemed good fun.

I got on particularly well with a secretary, Susan, who was slim, blonde, delicate, refined – all the things I wasn't. But we went most places together, and talked of going to Germany, to the beer festival. I never really believed I would go but I enjoyed talking about it, pretending.

As things turned out, the nearest I got to the German beer festival was Susan's birthday party where I began in good cheer and ended up in a psychiatric ward in Darwin. I got very drunk at the party and wandered off into the bush. That's all I remember. I was in the Darwin psychiatric ward for several days before Susan came to get me. She had with her a newspaper article about a missing woman – me – who had wandered into the bush at Rum Jungle. An Aboriginal tracker had found a shallow grave in the area but it turned out to be the carcass of a cow.

I remember going back to Rum Jungle with Susan but I don't remember staying there long; or how I left; or where I went. My next roll of photos was taken at Wyndham, where I worked as a waitress at the Swan Hotel.

It was a modern hotel, but life was much the same as any other pub: work, drink, sleep. I didn't like it much. One afternoon in the beer garden I got talking to a bloke called Keith. He had the weather-beaten face, the hat, the moleskins and boots of a cattleman. He represented the bush, horses, dogs – the life I wanted to live.

'I'm heading down to Meeka,' he said, 'then east to Wongawol Station, out along the Gunbarrel' – the treacherous dirt road 'highway' across the Gibson Desert. 'I'm the new manager out there. Got a stockman and a couple a dogs in tow. I need a cook though. Interested?'

'Sure,' I said. 'When are you leaving?'

'Few days, time for you to hand in your notice.'

So the three of us, and the dogs, travelled around the Great Sandy Desert and halfway through the Gibson Desert in a battered old station wagon, camped out all the way, and never had a wash during the whole trip. Bliss.

Keith's young stockman's name was Tom. I'm not sure whether he was half-caste or from down south, but he certainly didn't have the very dark skin or features of the Top End Aborigines. He was quiet and reserved, but had a good sense of humour and outlook on life. I liked him a lot. As we crashed along the inland 'road', over miles of corrugation, skidding through long hidden potholes and eating red dust, we sang all the good old songs: Slim Whitman's 'Rose Marie', 'Indian Love Call', 'China Doll'; Gene Autry's 'Tumbling Tumbleweeds', 'Don't Fence Me in' and 'Deep in the Heart of Texas'.

Wongawol Station is about 700 kilometres north of Kalgoorlie as the crow flies; semi-arid desert country, with an average rainfall of 25 centimetres per year and an evaporation rate of 30 centimetres per year.

One night I was out in the bough shed talking to Tom. We often had a bit of a chat after work. We ended up having sex. Word got around and Keith, who must have thought I would end up in his bed, was furious. He went into town, picked up a middle-aged white woman and brought her back to the station. She didn't do any work – she was there to be his bed warmer. I didn't care, but when she chucked her dirty undies in the washing I put them to one side; she could wash them herself. One morning Keith told me to wash her undies. When I refused he sacked me on the spot, and had me driven into town and dumped at the Wiluna Hotel. It was Christmas.

I was in the long bar, having a squash. It was hot and as he cooked the T-bones, sausages and mash, the cook had Bing Crosby moaning 'I'm Dreaming of a White Christmas' over and over. Outside, two F100s pulled up in a cloud of dust, and five men walked in. They ordered lunch and beers then racked the balls on the pool table.

'Play pool?' one of them asked.

'Yeah, thanks.'

'Live around here?'

'No, I've just come in from Wongawol. I'll go to Perth to look for a job soon.'

'Can you cook?'

'Sure.'

'Well, you've got a job! We're geologists, looking for nickel. We've got a camp, but not a cook.'

The camp was actually Milrose Station's shearers' quarters. The kitchen cupboards were all made of tin, hot to touch in summer, even before the wood stove was lit. The kitchen hadn't been used in months.

'Where have you been cooking?' I asked.

Howie, the head geologist, took me to one of the small worker's rooms. One side of it was lined with boxes of canned food, 'dog', stew, sausages and baked beans, Camp Pie. The other side was heaped up with empty cans. In the middle was a small primus with an unwashed pot on it and equally unwashed spoon. 'This is it!' Howie beamed proudly.

Howie and his wife Linda were from Canada, and the rest of his team was made up of an Italian, a Frenchman (who taught me how to cook crepes), two Brits, a New Zealander and an Aussie.

There were two kerosene fridges in the camp, but they never really got cold because the men were always stuffing hot beer into them. No room for food. I had to salt any meat we got from the station manager, then soak it and boil the hell out of it to make it edible.

Eventually the company, Falconbridge, had a large 240-volt generator sent up on a truck – no mean feat in that county – and a proper fridge and a freezer. From then on the food was flown in from Perth – Sara Lee cheesecakes, frozen chickens, the lot.

I liked the life out there and I was a bit put out when Larry, one of the big bosses from Canada who was visiting for a few days, told me I couldn't live out in the desert for the rest of my life.

'Why don't you go to town and put a dress on?'

'Because I don't want to.'

'Well, you'll have to go to Perth when the others take their six weeks off. You can't stay here on your own.'

'But what am I going to do in Perth?' I asked, already quite distressed.

'Do a course in something, improve yourself. You've got a good whack of money in your bank account now – use it wisely.'

I didn't want to do any of that, but because he was so 'fatherly' and seemed to care about my future, I didn't want to disappoint him.

Larry arranged for me to stay with his secretary, Norma, and do a telephonist/receptionist course. Soon I had a job in a small office. I worked for one morning, was sent out to get the lunches, then left. No one could understand why, and I couldn't either. I just knew I hated being there. I got a job as a pantry maid at the Transit Inn, a four star hotel in Central Perth. The job was much better, and I had to do something while waiting to go back to the desert. The people at the Transit Inn were good to me, teaching me different aspects of the job as I went along. But I was sliding into an unshakeable bout of depression. I needed to get away – run away, to be precise. I applied for a job as a cook on a sheep station up in the Gascoyne. I hadn't been in that area before, so was able to look forward to a change in life once my application was accepted. When I told Larry he organised a nice reference for me, the first I'd ever had. Then, at the age of twenty, I was on my way to Landor Station, my new home.

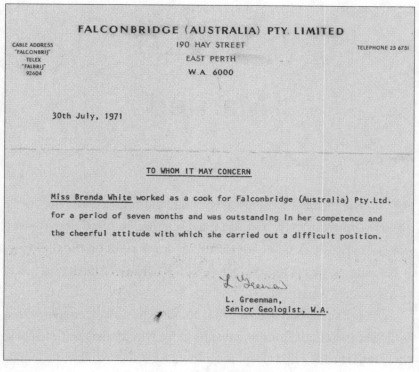

FALCONBRIDGE (AUSTRALIA) PTY. LIMITED

CABLE ADDRESS
"FALCONBRIJ"
TELEX
"FALBRIJ"
92604

190 HAY STREET
EAST PERTH
W.A. 6000

TELEPHONE 25 6751

30th July, 1971

TO WHOM IT MAY CONCERN

Miss Brenda White worked as a cook for Falconbridge (Australia) Pty.Ltd. for a period of seven months and was outstanding in her competence and the cheerful attitude with which she carried out a difficult position.

L. Greenman,
Senior Geologist, W.A.

Brenda Hodge's first reference

CHAPTER 11

Married

Landor was a comparatively small station: 350,000 hectares. Comparatively, because most holdings in that area are well over 400,000 hectares. But Landor is right on the Gascoyne River, and carries a lot of stock – 22,000 head of sheep and 3,000 cattle when I was there.

Landor's tin-roofed mud-brick homestead was extensive with a large verandah out front and enclosed fly-wired areas out the back, three dining rooms and sleeping quarters for visitors and white female staff. All the buildings, including the laundry, the meat-house and the men's quarters were painted white, with dark green trim. The gardens were beautiful; there was a small citrus orchard on the right-hand side of the house, and a large chook-run and vegie garden on the left. River gums created a tranquil atmosphere.

I used to start the day by getting the bread going, then making cribs (lunches) for the men who would be out all day. Breakfast was usually in two dining rooms – one for whites, one for blacks. After the dishes, I'd bake morning tea and afternoon tea in the one batch, cut up the cold meat for lunch, then start the washing. There was a washing-machine and a copper, so as well as housecleaning I could get quite a bit done before lunch. Lunch was easy, with not many mouths to feed.

After lunch I'd go out in the garden, or if it was very hot, have an afternoon siesta. After about 3 pm I'd start preparing the evening meal, set up all the tables, and make sweets. The evening meal was three-course: soup, mains and sweets. If Don had visitors up from Perth, he would sit at the head of the big table telling yarns, cracking jokes, and prolonging the service of food so that I sometimes didn't finish until 10 at night – a long day. That didn't bother Don, of course.

Don wasn't popular for various reasons, but when he shot himself in the head with a .44 handgun everyone remembered him as 'a good poor bastard'. I don't remember him as anything other than eccentric; he didn't give me any grief.

All the men were eccentric in some way, and all of them liked a prank. A couple of days after I arrived the overseer Richard asked me, 'Can you ride a horse?'

'A bit.' Did riding ponies bareback constitute the bushman's idea of riding a horse?

'We'll be running some horses in to get ready for the next muster today. You can come for a ride with us if you want.'

The horses were run into a large oval yard used for breaking them in. Waiting for me, saddled, was a nondescript bay gelding. As I walked up to get on, the bay eyeballed me and had his ears back. I should have guessed something was up: they were holding him right in the middle of the big yard, facing the gates, and stockmen, ready for the show and in high good humor, were perched up on the rails like cockatoos. I sat loose in the saddle and one of the boys ran to open the gates. As soon as the gates were open, the bay bucked –

bucked like hell – dumped me in the dirt and with reins and stirrups flapping, bolted through the gates. How I was going to take the joke? I'd been bucked from plenty of horses in my younger days; I didn't mind, and I was accepted after my initiation.

One morning I'd just taken a couple of slabs of fruit cake out of the oven when the 'roo shooter, David Hodge, called in for morning tea.

'What smells so good?' he asked, poking his head in the doorway, grinning from ear to ear.

'Cake,' I said nervously. 'Want some?'

He sort of stared at me, and I sort of stared at him... Unfortunately he already had a woman, Ina, a Mornington Islander. There were three children; an older girl about seven, Sonya about four, and Sandy, almost two.

Dave had built a house made of iron and louvres on the other side of a mud flat near the Aurillia Creek that ran into the Gascoyne River. I used to drive over to see Ina and the kids sometimes, and take them a cake or some bread. But I kept away from Dave because I felt guilty about being attracted to him. Then Ina left to go back to Queensland. She took the two girls with her, but left little Sandy with Dave. Because he had to shoot at night Dave would put Sandy on a blanket in a box in the cab of the Nissan. Not a satisfactory solution, which may be why he asked me to come out shooting sometime. Eventually I did, and that was it. The next day I shifted in with him. Dave was tall, built lean like a 'roo dog, a happy, friendly, quiet bloke: a bushy, as they say, and I loved him.

After a month or so Dave went to Mt Isa to find Sonya, his biological daughter. He found her. She was living off Cornflakes and powdered milk while her mother was in the pubs, and he brought her back. We married in Carnarvon, on 2 November 1972. I was 21, he was 34. We were together eight years.

The first four years were wonderful. We put the bore down and installed a pump, built a bough shed, fenced off a vegie garden and large chook pen, planted fruit trees and grape vines, and imported some Italian bees and a hive. For our honeymoon we went to Dubbo and then down to Melbourne to see my family. Nan was living at home with Jack and Edd at the time.

Nan had a new sewing-machine and was making herself some new clothes – short shorts and little sleeveless suits.

'Where are you going to wear those?' I asked, making conversation.

'It's hot over your way, isn't it? I'm coming over for a visit.' As usual, Nan didn't ask, she just made a declaration of her intent. I was angry. I didn't want her to come over. Outside I begged Dave: 'She's trouble, nothing but trouble!'

'She'll be sweet, she's your mother,' he said. 'The kids will enjoy having someone else around.'

'But Dave, you don't know her. She drinks like a fish and she starts bossing everyone around. Please!' Dave thought I was being unreasonable, so eventually I relented and told Nan she could come over if she didn't bring any grog. She promised she wouldn't. About a month later we got a message on the pedal set that she was in Meeka and waiting for someone to pick her up. Dave drove in – 250 kilometres – while I stayed home with the kids.

When he got back he was fuming. 'I nearly dumped her at Belele' (a station about 50 kilometres in from Meeka). He dropped her bags into the red dust. Straight away, by the size, shape and weight of one of her bags, I knew what the problem was. She had it loaded with cans of grog, and had been drinking most of the day. It occurred to me that as soon as they were out of town she'd probably put the hard word on him. But I didn't ask – I just knew that he was pretty upset.

When she had put down her suitcase and started packing her beer into our one small fridge we began to fight.

'You said you wouldn't bring any grog!' I said as I started taking the cans out again. 'We don't drink here, and I don't want you drinking in front of the kids!'

'Oh, come off it,' she smiled. 'One or two won't hurt, surely.'

Beaten, as always with Nan, I walked out of the vegie patch to calm down, did some watering, and left her to it. She only lasted a day. The next morning Dave packed her bags and drove her over to the station. She wore out her welcome over there too, and was told to be on the next mail truck to either Meeka or Carnarvon. The mail truck used to come every two weeks, and she caught the next one to Carnarvon. I didn't think Nan would stay there long – she was a big city bright lights woman. But she went back to using her first name Beryl, got a job at Carnarvon's Port Hotel and apparently made some good friends there over the years.

'She was mad, but good fun,' one of these friends, Shirley Lester, told me when I went back to find out how my mother spent her last years. I was glad to hear she'd been able to relax and enjoy her later years. She'd always said that was what she wanted to do.

We were happy enough on Landor, but things happened that convinced Dave it was time to move on. American animal rights groups lobbied successfully to ban kangaroo products from entering America, and the 'roo industry went into decline. When the Federal Government reduced the number of tags (one tag per 'roo) in any one licence from about 10,000 to 1,000 it made shooting uneconomic. We were barely making enough to pay the petrol bill.

Dave and I wanted to send the kids to school so they could learn and mix with other kids – being black they needed all the opportunities they could get and there wasn't anything for them on the station – so that meant a move.

And there was Don's death. Dave had made a gentleman's agreement with Don that if Dave wanted to leave Don would pay him for the labour and materials involved in building our house and the outbuildings. After Don died, his brother Bob came over to supervise the muster of sheep and shearing but he refused to pay Dave anything. Dave was about to see a lawyer when Bob and the overseer were killed in a light-plane crash.

Dave sold a small investment property he had in Geraldton, and bought a 20-hectare farm at Mt Helena, in the foothills of Perth. We loaded the Nissan with fuel drums, wire, pipes, motors and all sorts of men's junk, and towed a double horse float with my horse, two sheep and bails of hay. I drove the old Holden, packed to the roof with Sonya and Sandy, clothes, personal belongings, two dogs and two cats.

We tried to make our new home self-sufficient. There were half a dozen milking cows on the place when we bought it, and we put a young Poll-Hereford bull in with them to produce meat calves. There was a piggery down the back and we put in large white sows and a boar and fed them the skim milk which was left after separation. We sold cream and made butter with the rest, and we put 30 sheep in the bottom paddock.

We had chooks for eggs, grew our own vegies and the rest we bought in bulk from Elders in Perth, so there was no need to go shopping on a daily or weekly basis.

Dave and I worked well together and things would have been a lot better if he hadn't had to spend so much time working as a fencing contractor and yard builder, away for days at a time. I did the everyday jobs – looking after the kids, the housework, cooking, fruit-bottling, chopping wood for the stove, milking, feeding the pigs, gardening and riding my old horse from the station.

It was a good, healthy life, but when Sonya started school she became unsettled, and I didn't know how to deal with it. She had been badly neglected by her mother when they were in Mt Isa, but unlike young Sandy, who was always happy, never complained, and never cried, Sonya missed her mother. You may find that hard to understand, but I can: I too, missed my mother, now and again. And Sonya must have felt out of place in a predominantly white school, in a strange area, and with very little parental support. I tried to help her with her school work, but the system was foreign to me: arithmetic was done with beads on bars, and spelling and punctuation were not to be corrected because, her teacher explained, it would 'ruin' her flow of thought and expression.

Sonya started stealing things from her classmates and tipping sand down petrol tanks. She set fire to our farm in the middle of summer (luckily there was little to burn) and once she tried to run away, taking Sandy with her. I took to belting her when she wouldn't do as I asked – not as savagely as my mother belted me, but too harshly nonetheless. I would lose my temper with her, hit her, then feel scared and guilty about what I'd done, triggering another bout of depression. I kept working when I was depressed but didn't eat much, and often passed out – I'd stop breathing, then hyperventilate, gasping for air. This was no excuse for hitting children – history was repeating itself and I should have sought professional help.

I don't know where Sonya or Sandy are today; I haven't seen or heard of them since 1977. I hope they have had good lives since then. Dave loved them both, and I can only apologise for my shortcomings as a stepmother.

Both the kids went to school at Mt Helena and I started work part-time at a greengrocer's in Sawyer's Valley. I made sure the kids were never home alone after school, and I still had to do the farm work, morning and afternoon. But things between Dave and me were going sour. I didn't want to have the responsibility of bringing up his children (I was doing such a bad job of it), and I couldn't be bothered much with sex, after working from 4 am till 8 or 9 pm each day. Dave was a workaholic – he could work all day and half the night and still get up before the sun. I was only in my 20s, but I had trouble keeping up with it all.

At some time, Dave started 'visiting' a friend of mine whose kids went to the same school as ours. Sandy let the cat out of the bag after a trip to the bush with his father.

'Steven said we have to go back to school soon.'

'Oh yeah? When did you see Steven?'

'Umm… yesterday, after work. Daddy goes there for a cuppa tea.'

I hate being lied to, but I didn't confront him about it; I don't like argument. We just grew further and further apart, until one afternoon he put some papers on the kitchen table and asked me to sign them.

'What are they?'

'I've been to see a lawyer, I want you to sign your share of property back to me.'

I was shattered, but I choked out: 'Well if that's how much you think of our marriage, you can stick it up your arse! As soon as I get somewhere else to live, you won't see me for dust!'

There were nasty moments between us in the following weeks. I started sleeping around. I shifted into the spare room. Dave made sure I didn't get any sleep when he was home, slamming doors, and switching my bedroom light on at all hours of the night. I was scared of him. Eventually I got a live-in job at Jane Brook stud in Middle

Swan, just out of Perth, and moved out with the old Holden, a horse float and my horses. Strangely enough, I didn't miss Dave or the kids when I left. I had 'escaped' – yet again – and I had a job. That was all I cared about.

CHAPTER 12

Divorced

Jane Brook stud was a deceased estate – the Stratton estate – now part of a suburb called Stratton. It was managed by Bill Ornsby. A horseman who had spent many years on the rodeo circuit, Bill was a respected breeder of thoroughbreds and pacers, and a renowned judge of many breeds at the agricultural shows. I admired Bill because he cared as much about temperament as confirmation in breeding stock. He knew more than most about horses: without a whip or a rope in his hand he could eyeball a youngster until it faced up to him, and soon accepted the bridle and harness. I loved being on the stud, working with mares and foals, preparing yearlings for the sales, and showing my own horses on weekends. I had two Appaloosa mares I had bought while I was with Dave and bred some lovely foals from them. I sold one yearling colt for $5,000 and got out of debt. Rain, hail or shine, my life revolved around horses for the next five years.

I worked six and a half days a week, and went to the pub's Sunday session on my half day off. It was at one of these sessions I met Gordon.

I was drinking at a table on my own; he was with a group of young people. I thought, as he walked up to me, that he was a lout. He had on blue jeans, a bikie T-shirt, and wild wavy black hair. We got on instantly. I was 28 and he was 24. We spent that summer at sessions, swimming at the river, going to the drive-in, and at the end of it we got a unit and lived together. We were both divorced, and neither of us wanted to get married again.

I kept working the same hours with the horses, and Gordon had a job at the old Midland brick – stacking from the old kilns, arduous work, but it pays well.

Every year, for four years, with a convoy of dune-buggy and dirt-bike enthusiasts' girlfriends, wives and kids, we went away camping up to Lancelin, on the coast about 150 kilometres north of Perth. There's a good pub right on the water's edge at Lancelin, where we could always get a great seafood basket, but most of the time we cooked what we'd caught that day, fried in the pan or grilled over a fire, washed down with wine or beer from an Esky. Good times and good people.

One night I had a phone call from Melbourne. It was Jack. Edd was in a coma, he said, in intensive care, at Box Hill Hospital. I borrowed from Bill Ornsby and flew over the next day. Jack was still at the old Doncaster home, Number 29 as we called it. I found him pacing up and down the lounge room, crying, muttering. He'd been drinking whisky and not eating. After ten years of looking after Edd, who had severe epilepsy, Jack needed looking after himself. I felt so sorry for him. Then I saw Edd in the intensive care unit and I broke down. Edd was so pale I thought he was dead. His breathing was assisted. He didn't move.

Jack and I walked the five kilometres home that night. We needed to feel the cold air, to keep moving, to do something in the face of such overwhelming helplessness. I had to go back to Perth after a few days, but I returned to Melbourne after Edd recovered and persuaded him to come to live in Perth with Gordon and me in our two-bedroom duplex in Midland. I was a bit worried about Jack being on his own, but as it turned out he started having a social life for the first time in years, falling in love with a woman at the footy club and starting a new life with her. I knew Edd would get on well with Gordon – everyone did – and specialists eventually got his medication good enough to stablise him.

It took a while for Edd to get his coordination back, and he still had the odd fit, but all we had to do was get him back on his feet – a driver's licence and a job. Edd did all the footwork, finally landing himself a job at the old Midland Railyards. He could have done clerical work – he used to be a clerk at Russell Street Police Headquarters in Melbourne – but he wanted to do something different, so he started in the workshops as an assistant, and ended up in charge of a team of twelve men and some modernised machinery from America. Edd worked at Midland Railways for fourteen years, until the Court Government sacked 900 workers and eventually closed it down.

Bill Orsnby and I went out drenching horses on a farm up at Gidgegannup one day. 'Do you know anyone who wants a pup?' asked the farmer's wife. 'If I don't get rid of them before my husband gets back next week, he's going to knock them.' We had a look at the pups – eight black and white blue-heeler cross kelpies about six weeks old. One of them was huge, and much heavier than the rest. 'Must have a rat in the woodpile here,' I ventured.

'Yes,' she said, 'he's the odd one out and no one wants him.'

I immediately wanted him. I also took a little bitch to keep him company while I was at work. Gordon and Edd were impressed. 'What'll we call them?'

'Boris and Doris,' I said. 'If we call one, they'll both come.' They were gorgeous pups, but like all pups they liked to dig holes. The backyard looked like a rabbit warren. The owner of the duplex, an Italian man, did an inspection while I was at work. 'You got dogs,' he thundered, 'they gotta go!'

'But they're only pups... we'll fill in the holes.'

'You don't get rid of them, I get rid of you!'

'In that case, we're moving out – you can stick it!'

Feeling self-righteous and superior I got home and told the boys. They were horrified – I could tell by the look on their faces – but they said nothing.

'Don't worry, I'll find a place that takes dogs.' After a week I was getting worried. At the last minute we got an old derelict mansion down on the river. The floorboards wobbled and the walls came away from the roof in places, but it was such a big old house there was still plenty of room to live quite comfortably.

Gordon's parents were very good to us. They lived in Rockingham, south of Perth on the coast. They used to take us all out fishing in their boat, even Jack when he came over for holidays. Gordon is their only child, so it's probably a disappointment to them that he wasted the best years of his young life – he was 28 by then – with someone who was infertile and moody, but they never showed it. Even after I was sent to prison Gordon's mum sent me cards and let me know how they were going. They are lovely people, and I still don't know today why I ever left Gordon. It was a big mistake.

After five years I became agitated; I needed to 'get away' again. I left my job, Gordon, Edd, my horses – everything. I packed up my panel van and a trailer and with my dog Boris headed east over the Nullarbor. I remember hurtling across the tree-less plains, driving like the devil, with 'Nights in White Satin' blaring from my cassette player while Boris put his paws over his ears.

I can't remember whether I went to Melbourne. But I know I missed Sydney and went up the Newell Highway and straight through Brisbane and Townsville for Cairns. Why? Because I hadn't been there before. I still had this irrational belief that a new place would be 'good', that I would be happy there. I was now in my thirties, and I still didn't know why I became so unhappy, why I cried 'for no reason', why I could never find a place where I felt I belonged.

I picked up a German backpacker along the way, who introduced me to marijuana. We toured up the far north Queensland coast, slept on the beaches, swam when we wanted to, ate mouth-watering fresh fruit, and smoked dope as the sun set on tranquil waters. It was idyllic, but emotionally I was still on the run. I packed up and drove alone across the Top End again. I just kept on driving. When I ran out of money I would work for a few weeks, usually in pubs counter cooking, then head off again.

Darwin had been rebuilt and expanded after Cyclone Tracy. I didn't recognise much of it. I'd loved it the first time I was there, but this time it was just another city full of strangers. I thought all the places I revisited had changed, but actually it was me who had changed. I was desperately looking for happiness outside myself, my inner-self being in turmoil and in denial. I was, as someone once told me, like a duck on water, gliding along on the surface, but paddling like hell underneath.

I drove over to Derby, got a job through an agency as a station cook at Rosewood, up near Lake Argyle (1,200 kilometres back from where I'd just come), and worked there for a few months until the muster was finished and 'the wet' was due to start. All seasonal workers – including me – had to go. Meanwhile, Gordon had come up north and was working on a station the other side of Halls Creek.

I called in to see him. He was clearing out before the wet season as well, so we travelled back to Derby together, then did a 'beach crawl' back to Perth.

Edd was getting on okay, still working and happy to be independent again, renting a nice house at the foot of the Darling Ranges. Gordon and I stayed at the Caversham caravan park for a while, and it was a stressful time. Gordon was so nice, so easy to get along with, asking me quietly if we could get back together again. Maybe I was just too used to being pushed around, a life pattern in which being given freedom of choice becomes abnormal. I cried a lot and told him I didn't want to stay with him. I hated hurting him that way – I still regret it very much.

CHAPTER 13

'I've Shot a Man'

It was getting dark as I parked my van outside the Kalgoorlie police station. Inside, there was only one officer, middle-aged, at the front desk. A kind man, I remember thinking later.

'Help you?'

'Um… I've shot a man.'

'Is he dead?'

'I don't know.'

'Who is this man?'

'Sergeant Peter Rafferty… he works here…'

He took me to a small office space and pulled out a seat. 'Just wait here, I'll get someone to look after you…' he said, and there I was, sitting staring at a red binder-file, the word RAFFERTY printed on its spine.

I had met Peter Rafferty in Leonora, a small mining town 140 kilometres north of Kalgoorlie. After I left Gordon, I drove up to Meekathana, heading north again, but on the way I was offered a job as a roadhouse cook at Leonora.

Leonora was a small place in 1983. One main street, an Elders store, a general store, a garage, a roadhouse, a small library, three pubs – one closed – and around 400 whites and as many Aboriginals in various camps just out of town. A large part of the town's economy was based on Aboriginal welfare money. They were not treated well in that town.

Peter had been sent up as a relief sergeant at the same time as I arrived in Leonora. We met in the main street, and struck it off right away. I liked him. Open, friendly, and down to earth, he cared about people, especially the Aboriginal people.

But he drank. Sometimes Peter would get into a kind of silent stupor, then vomit spontaneously wherever he was. I never saw him do this in public, however, and because he wasn't violent towards me I didn't see any harm in it – apart from what it was doing to his health. Most of the time, he appeared to be sober, and he was enthusiastic, active, and a lot of fun to be with. He boarded in the town. I lived in an old abandoned house out at Gwalia, a ghost town at the time. I shared with one of my workmates, Anne, a bubbly, hard-working, hard-playing girl in her early 20s who liked watching videos, smoking dope and playing pool at the pub.

Peter spent a lot of time at one of the town's two hotels, especially at night when he wasn't on duty. He was an unofficial bouncer, I think, but there was seldom any trouble in the white's drinking areas.

Gary Rokich drove into Leonora one day as I was walking down the main street. He stopped and asked me for directions, but didn't introduce himself. I met him again at the main pub on a Friday night, where I was having a few quiet drinks with Peter. Peter used to spend a lot of his off-duty nights there, and I think he had some sort of private deal going with the proprietress. As the police sergeant in a small town, his presence was seen to deter troublemakers whether he was in uniform or not. We were with half a dozen others in the lounge and I went over to the jukebox to put on some more songs. Gary walked in, came straight over to me and asked if I wanted a drink – probably because I was the only familiar face he could see. When I went back to our table Peter frowned.

'Who's that?'

'I don't know,' I shrugged. 'He's new in town. He asked me to have a drink, but I told him I'm with you.' Peter said nothing.

I had to work in the morning and I went home and was asleep long before pub closing time. I was woken by a phone call. Peter wanted to see me; he'd been in a fight. I drove back into town, to the place where he was boarding. The lights were on, music was playing, and lots of people were there. It looked like a party. Peter was inside, drinking, nursing a black eye. When I asked him what happened he wouldn't say. He just seemed to want to be surrounded by people.

Recently, twenty years later, I contacted Gary Rokich. He had gone to Perth before my trial, and when asked to come back to Kalgoorlie as a Crown witness he refused, he told me, because he didn't like what Peter had done to him. Gary told me that after I left the hotel in Leonora that night Peter, who wasn't in uniform, approached him three times and abused him for talking to me and Anne. The third time, Gary invited him to step outside, where Gary punched him in the eye. Peter came back with uniformed officers. They took Gary to the lock-up and gave him a hiding before Peter charged him with aggravated assault.

Peter and I had only known each other for a couple of months when he was transferred back to Kalgoorlie. He wanted me to go with him, and because I wanted to be wanted, I did. I left my job and followed

Man fined over hotel incident

A Kalgoorlie man was fined $150 in the Leonora Court of Petty Sessions when he pleaded guilty to charges arising from an incident at a Leonora Hotel last weekend.

Garry Rokich (32), an electrical supervisor, was charged with being disorderly by creating a disturbance at the hotel and with aggravated assault.

The court was told that the police were called to the hotel last Friday evening and on arrival, one of the policemen was struck in the face by Rokich.

The officer received severe bruising to his eye.

Rokich was fined $50 for creating a disturbance and a further $100 for assaulting the police officer.

FROM *THE KALGOORLIE MINER*

him to Kalgoorlie, where we rented a home together. He lined up a job for me, cooking at The Star and Garter hotel-motel. The manager's wife was very good to me, and, after I went to prison, sent me wages still owing. Most people ripped me off, took what little I had – including a Mitsubishi van – once the news hit the papers. At the time I didn't care, I didn't care about anything. But looking back I can see that some people, like the manager's wife, are just basically honest and decent, no matter what the circumstances. These are the people who have taught me values, not by what they say but by what they do.

Peter had a pacer in work, and a couple of other horses. He kept them stabled at the track initially, while we turned an old shed and lean-to into stables and tack room at the place we were renting. Peter would gear up his horse and drive it straight into the track from there. Sometimes I exercised it under saddle, when he was on late shifts. He took me to the trots and out prospecting. We did most things together. But he had his friends and I had mine.

Anne and her boyfriend had also shifted to Kal from Leonora, and I went over to their place when I had time. Sometimes Anne came to the Star and Garter to play pool, and I'd have a drink with her after work. If I stayed for more than one drink, Peter's friend from the Liquor and Gaming or somebody else would invariably turn up to keep an unofficial eye on me. When I was home on my own at night there would be a police car parked in the vacant land across from our house – for hours. In the daytime police cars would cruise up the back alley if there was no sign of me in the front garden. Sometimes Peter would send a young constable to our house to 'pick up some paper work' he said he'd forgotten. I suppose it might sound very endearing that he was so concerned for me, but the fact was I was under surveillance.

As Peter's drinking got worse, he became more dementedly jealous. He sent me to the bottle shop to get him a carton one day. It was a five-minute walk away, and I was back within 15 minutes, carrying the beer. From the front verandah he called out. 'Where have you been? Rooting the bloke at the bottle shop?'

It wasn't long before these kind of mind games made me nervous, and deeply depressed. I didn't realise that he was having alcoholic delusions, that sometimes when he accused me of things he thought I was his ex-wife. At this point I should have sought professional help, but I'd never done that before and it didn't occur to me to start. Peter said he'd been to see a doctor, but he wasn't taking any medication for chest pains and he was frequently vomiting.

I was beginning to feel trapped.

One night I was cleaning my rifle – a licensed .22 – when Peter went through some of his boxes in the spare room and brought out a clear container half full of ammunition and a scope.

'Where's your rifle?' I asked.

He grinned. 'Hidden away.' Then he went on to tell me that the police down south had taken it off him, but he had stolen it back from a police station. We had an old wooden wardrobe in the spare room which was always locked. I presumed he kept his rifle in there. But I never saw it and didn't even think about it at the time. He left the ammunition on a bench in the kitchen, for what purpose I don't know. Months later, when I was in prison, a female officer told me she knew Peter's ex-wife, that he had threatened her with his rifle after their separation, and the police had confiscated it. I was told she took out a restraining order on him, which is why he was transferred to Kalgoorlie.

Whatever the case, I believed he had a rifle hidden in the house on the day I decided to leave him.

For weeks before that day I had severe depression. It started when someone from the force in Perth rang Peter at night and told him things that got him angry. He started making other calls to Perth, one, I think, to his ex-wife. Whoever it was, he got even more stirred up. Instead of minding my own business, I stupidly said, 'You seem to enjoy all this family drama.' That put him in a rage. He yelled at me, I yelled back at him. He stormed out of the house and drove away. Our relationship was never good after that. I couldn't get Peter to talk things out. He wanted to just pretend everything was okay even though we both knew it wasn't.

I couldn't stop crying at work, I couldn't stop crying at home, I could hardly get out of bed in the mornings to face the day. I soon turned to Anne for help. Smoking dope seemed the only way to deaden my pain.

Peter took to the bottle to deaden his pain. I found him drinking on his own out in the stables one night, muttering to himself. When I asked if he was all right he just spat at me, 'You never cared about the kids – all you care about is money!'

An emotional mess, I drove over to Anne's place and stayed with them for the night. When I went back the next morning, Peter was in bed, wide awake, staring at the roof. I offered to make him a cup of tea, but he wouldn't talk to me. When he got dressed and went out the back to get one of the horses ready for track work, I asked him, 'What do you want me to do, stay or go?' He ignored me totally, as if I wasn't there.

It is difficult enough to recall a sequence of events that happened twenty years ago, but more so when those events were impaired by short-term memory loss, as they were happening. Immediately after Peter's death, when detectives were questioning me, my memory was only partial and disjointed. There was a whole day I could not account for – I think it was the Friday. I'm sure this memory loss was mainly brought on by emotional trauma – what one professional told me was 'hysterical fugue' – but the amount of dope I had smoked may have also been a contributing factor.

Whatever the case, six years later, I wrote all I could remember of the events leading up to Peter's death in an appeal for mercy to the governor of Western Australia. I reproduce part of that appeal here as it stands, because I can't add anything to it in terms of explaining what happened.

After giving Peter the cup of tea, and realising that he wasn't going to talk to me, I went outside to do my work: water the garden, feed the horses, clean the yards. After a while Peter came out and started gearing up one of the mares we had in work (we lived opposite the trotting track). I tried a direct approach and asked, 'Do you want me to stay with you or not?' After a long pause he just said, 'You can do what you like' or something to that effect. I needed to know whether he wanted me with him or not, but further questioning was met with a sullen silence, and then he drove off. By this time I was depressed (in the clinical sense, as I now understand it). I had been crying off and on all night and had hardly slept at all. So I reverted to the only coping strategy I knew: I went bush. (I should have gone to someone to talk the problem out, but had grown up being told not to whinge, complain, or seek sympathy when upset.) I drove out to the bush and walked around out there for a long time, trying to think, but I was very confused, upset and tired. Eventually I went back to try to talk to Peter again. When I got home there was a note on the kitchen table inviting me to meet him at the hotel for a drink. I was shocked; it was as though he thought that nothing had happened. I decided not to go because I didn't want to be seen with red, puffy eyes, and because I just didn't have the energy.

At some stage during that day Anne and her boyfriend came around and asked me to come and have a look at the house they were shifting into. I think it was the same day, but I'm not sure. Anyway, they were trying to cheer me up, but I was not good company, and soon went home again. Some time later, Peter came back. He asked me if I wanted a drink (alcohol), and I said yes. I was sitting on the front porch and he just stood there staring at me. It was very unnerving when he did that. I said something about my young brother, that I would tell him not to come up to stay with us for his Easter holidays if Peter was going to continue acting as he had been. That was not very tactful either, as it set him off again. He went inside and started yelling at me. I started screaming at him and smashed my glass down on the footpath. Then I ran into the bedroom crying hysterically. By this time my head was pounding and I couldn't stop shaking. I went back out to him at some stage, and he started yelling about the kids and the money, called me a slut and a whore, and let loose a tirade of abuse – all of which I took personally. I should have known from the first time this happened that he was looking at me, but seeing his ex-wife. However I was highly emotional myself at that stage, and not thinking clearly.

At one stage I said to Peter that I would be leaving him as soon as the rent I had already paid ran out – which would have been in another one and a half weeks' time. I knew I had to leave, but a part of me kept hoping that things would get better before then. As it turned out, he ordered me to leave the house immediately, and kept following me around as I was packing, rushing me, as though he couldn't wait to get rid of me. This devastated me. I was too emotionally exhausted by that time to even cry anymore.

As I started putting my things into my van, I realised that I would have to make two trips. Peter was in a very nasty mood, and he said that if I didn't return from the first trip within *exactly* 20 minutes he would throw all the rest of my gear out onto the road. He kept pointing to his watch and repeating this, although he then said he would throw all my gear into the paddock next door (which was a favourite drinking spot of some Aboriginal people). My possessions were not worth a lot of money, but they were all I had. They were, at that time, my identity: my books, some saved from childhood; and my camping, gardening and horse gear. I can see ways of getting around this situation now, but I couldn't at the time. I reverted to my childhood mode of being: when the dominant parent gives an order, the child does not question but *must* obey. I drove off in a daze, knowing only that I must be back in 20 minutes.

No one was home when I arrived at Anne's place, so I climbed in through a back window, opened the door, and just started piling my clothes and things in the kitchen. During the unpacking the bottom drawer of my first-aid kit slid open and I saw the loaded clip of my rifle there. I had forgotten all about it up until then, but when I saw it I took my rifle from the van (where I always kept it when travelling), loaded it with the clip, and put it back in the front of my van. When Dave and I were in the bush, we always had a loaded rifle in the vehicle – but in a safe position. My .22 was licensed; I was a licensed shooter (N.T.), and I suppose I just felt safer having the rifle with me. I don't really know why I loaded it and took it back to our house because I was not thinking about anything, I was just feeling the urgency of having to be back within 20 minutes (as though the world would end if I didn't). I realise that this will sound very unlikely given the events that followed, but it is true. During the trip back I was in a worse sort of daze. I remember that I went straight through a busy intersection and nearly crashed with another vehicle, which had to brake hard to miss me. I felt as though I was floating (a difficult feeling to put into words) and I didn't even care that I had nearly smashed into another car. When I say I didn't care, I mean that I didn't get a fright or worry about the possible consequences as I would have normally.

When I pulled up at the front of the house, Peter was sitting on the porch, still drinking (he could put away a lot of beer without outwardly showing the effects of it). He just sat there staring at me, saying nothing. I had a large drum of horse gear that I could not shift, so I had to empty it and carry everything in small lots. Peter didn't offer to help; he just sat there staring at me. Then I had to drive around to the back to pick up more horse rugs and gardening tools. When I drove into the back yard, Peter ran out of the house abusing me again. He must have known it was me at that time because some of the things he said he knew would hurt me personally. I tried to ignore him, walking back and forth to the van with gear, not answering him. He was following me back and forth, abusing me, taunting me, and whether intentional or not, provoking me. I believe he was provoking me because he seemed to be trying everything possible (bar physical violence) to get me to break down completely. I had the same treatment from my ex-husband on several occasions during our separation (until the property settlement), although he was not a drinking man.

V. Description of the Offence

This is the most difficult part, not only because it still upsets me, but because my memory is only of images; and those images were not, at the time, associated to any meaning. Also, the images are fragmentary, not continuous, but I think the order is fairly accurate. The images that I can remember, that is, colours, forms and minor sensations, are still very vivid in my mind. However, because of the time lapse of six years, and because it was an abnormal experience, I acknowledge that there may be some impairment to my memory in this recollection.

The last thing I remember Peter saying is, 'You are mad, do you know that?' After that, I couldn't hear anything – not even the sound of the rifle being fired – until I heard Boris barking after I had shot Peter several times. The first sensation I remember after Peter's remark was a very soft sort of whirring in my ears; but all other noises – traffic, birds, wind – had stopped. At the same time, my movement felt very slow. I remember walking around to the front of the van and getting my rifle out; the only analogy I can think of for my movement is a slow version of how astronauts walk on the moon – that floating feeling again, but slowed right down. Then I was standing on the other side of the van, and Peter was inside the feed shed, with the top half of his body visible through an open space in the shed. He was facing me, staring at me, not moving, not speaking. I remember trying to call out, 'Come out here' (for what purpose I don't know, because he was not far away from me anyway), and I think I did say that, but I couldn't hear my own words. I seemed to be standing there for ages, staring at Peter's blue form – which was like a statue, I mean really like a statue. I was looking at Peter, but I was not seeing Peter as a person. When I shot at him I did not think to myself, 'You are the man who has been tormenting me and I am going to shoot you.' I didn't think anything; I just did it. I can remember raising the rifle to my shoulder, and taking aim, and (maybe) pulling the trigger. Then there was a period when all I could see was blackness – even though my eyes were open. When the blackness passed, I was looking at the back of the bolt, the rifle still raised to my shoulder. This is very unusual, because I had been trained to keep my eye on the sights in order to see where the 'roo had been shot (I will go into this training in the next section, VI). I do remember working the bolt, but I have no memory of the sound of the shots. At one stage – after another gap in memory – I was standing close to the outside of the shed and was looking directly into the afternoon sun (my head tilted up). I remember the colours, yellow, white, orange, but did not feel any burning sensation in my eyes. I seemed to be rooted to the spot, mesmerised by the sun;

147

but I can't have been looking at it for too long or my eyes would have been damaged. Another gap in memory – then I was standing outside the door to the feed shed, and I could see Peter's blue shirt through the gap between the door and the frame. Again, I did not think of him as Peter, or as anyone. I felt nothing. As I think I said to my counsel, it was worse than nothing. It was more nothingness than the normal sense of saying that we feel nothing. I had not experienced it before, and have not experienced it since. It is a terrible thing to have to admit that I shot Peter in his refuge through the door gap, and in the back, but that is what I did. He fell forwards and sideways, close to the doorway, and I must have moved forward a bit and shot him in the head (the forensic reports say at close range). The rifle must have been already pointing downwards; all I know is that I kept on shooting. For what purpose, I keep asking myself, if not to kill? I only know that I have no memory of wanting to kill Peter, or of shooting for a purpose at all.

Suddenly, I heard Boris barking. I hadn't seen or heard him until that moment, but then he was there, snapping at Peter's head and barking loudly. That was when my movements felt normal again, and when time lost its distortion. I just walked to my van, put the rifle in it, and drove off. Some people were playing tennis at the back of our place, and I remember feeling annoyed because they were laughing. The only other feelings I had were that I wanted to get away from Peter, and I had a sudden very demanding thirst. I drove straight to the local deli where I bought and drank a bottle of cool drink. I then went to a hotel (I don't know which one) and drank rum and coke for a while; then I went and sat on a hill which overlooks Kalgoorlie for I don't know how long; then I went to the police station and told the duty officer that I had shot a man.

I have never seen a copy of the trial transcript, and I have not seen a copy of my statement since the time of the trial, so if the above sequence of events deviates from earlier evidence, I can't help that. I can only recount what happened as I remember it now.

As to my abnormal state of mind during the shooting, I have since been told by prison psychologist, Mr Paul McEvoy, that what I experienced was a temporary dissociation disorder, similar to battle fatigue in soldiers. This analogy is relevant because, after living with Peter for three or four months, I felt as though I was living in a battlefield. The increasing intensity of the tensions between us, and of my confusion and distress in our last month together, left me emotionally and physically exhausted.

VI. A Recent Observation on My Use of the Rifle

I must first say that the observation I am about to make might be interpreted as a legal issue, but I do not want to raise it as a legal issue. Again, I am only concerned with trying to explain what happened.

VIII. I was instructed by my counsel for trial not to mention that my ex-husband was a professional shooter because he thought it might give people the idea that I know how to use a rifle. I did not question this (or anything else) at the time, and did as I was told. However, I do know how to use a rifle – very accurately. I worked alongside my husband for two years when he was shooting professionally, during which time he trained me to shoot to kill instantly. (He refused to leave a wounded animal hopping around the bush, and he was very conscious of the time and costs involved in trying to find a wounded animal at night.) Therefore, if I had been in control of my actions when I shot Peter, and if I had meant to kill him, I would have done so with the first shot. It seems to me that my earlier training explains how I used the rifle automatically, that is, without thinking about what I was doing – although it still doesn't explain why I used it.

Looking back it is interesting now that I was advised by my counsel to delete any mention of my husband being a 'roo shooter because 'It might give people the idea I know how to use a rifle.' It seems to me that if I didn't know how to use a rifle I wouldn't have had both a licensed firearm and a shooter's licence.

Coincidentally, Ronald Ryan, hanged at Melbourne in 1967, was also described as making 'his biggest mistake' by saying under oath that his job in life was 'roo shooter. The prosecution seized on this: "Roo shooters are good shots aren't they?' This is an example of how 'the truth', our holy grail in Christian and democratic countries, is so often sought, discovered, then rejected in courts of law simply because 'it doesn't look good'.

As I mentioned earlier, I had no sense of time, so I don't know how long I had been in the yard. After hearing Boris barking at Peter, the next thing I remember is driving out through the back gates in my van. My coordination and hearing had returned, but I was still 'numb' in the mind. The thing I remember most is feeling very, very thirsty. Why I didn't go to the tap and have a drink, I don't know.

I drove towards town, stopped at a deli, and bought a bottle of Coke. I hate Coke but I had an unquenchable thirst. A policeman in uniform pulled up and came into the shop. I just stared at him, half thinking he would take me to prison, but all he did was buy some smokes and walk out. I watched him drive off, feeling nothing.

I drove on a bit further, then pulled up at a hotel. There was loud music somewhere. I went in and bought a drink, sat down at an empty table, and waited for the police to come and get me.

'Hi! Remember me?' Gary Rokich, the man who had inadvertently ignited the smouldering jealousy of Peter, was standing, looking down at me. I didn't answer.

'Are you okay?' Leaning down, looking at me closely.

'No, I'm not.'

'What's wrong? What's happened?'

'I shot Peter.'

'Oh yeah! Right!... You're joking... aren't you?'

I walked out, and never saw him again.

The next thing I remember is being up at a lookout somewhere close to the main streets of Kalgoorlie. I sat up there for ages until it finally occurred to me that the police were not coming to get me. I thought about shooting myself, but just kept sitting there, watching the day come to an end. The next thing I remember is parking outside the police station and walking in.

I don't know how long the questioning went on for – several hours I think. Sometimes they asked me the same thing over and over. One of those questions was, 'Did you mean to kill him?'

'Well, I suppose I must have… it wasn't an accident,' I'd say. By that, I meant that I didn't trip over and discharge the firearm. A shooting accident usually happens when people are climbing over fences or getting down from vehicles with a loaded gun. But what the detectives wanted to know was whether or not I had intent at the time of the shooting, so my answers were self-incriminating.

I was taken out to my van and photographed. I was fingerprinted, then put in the lock-up. There were several Aboriginal women in the yard. I was given a blanket and cell off to the side. When everything went quiet I pulled the blanket over my head and was finally able to have a proper cry. And when I couldn't cry anymore, I just lay there, looking at the wall I was facing, thinking vaguely about the brick walls I used to stare at in Winlaton nearly twenty years earlier.

Looking forward another twenty years, I now have relative peace and happiness – but in 1984 I had no vision of a future, I felt like a dead man walking. I didn't know anything about sentencing and prisons in those days, but I was somehow confident within myself that I would be hung. Maybe it came from my mother's old threat: 'They hang horse thieves in this country, you know!'

What was going on in my mind? I don't know. I was exhausted.

Two men came to the cell door at one stage and one of them said, 'Hmph! Sleeping like a baby.' He thought I didn't care about what I'd done to Peter. But I wasn't asleep. I was hiding in the dark under my one blanket, crying to myself, not wanting to see or talk to anyone. I did sleep, later on, and was woken early in the morning to a pannikin of warm black tea.

CHAPTER 14

Court and Remand

After a court appearance I was taken to Boulder Regional Prison and locked in one of two isolation or 'security' cells. Relatively modern – hang-proof, in other words – each had a small exercise yard with mesh above through which the sky could be seen. I was put in the right-hand cell, and a young Aboriginal woman, Jenna Lynch, was in the other. I couldn't see her, but I could hear her music sometimes. We became good friends over the next 12 months. She too had shot and killed her husband, but she never spoke of it. I didn't care why she was there; I appreciated her quiet, often silent, company and it was comforting to know I was not alone in my tomb.

Jenna and I, a few weeks later, were taken 600 kilometres to Bandyup, on the outskirts of Perth, the only women's prison in Western Australia. Bundled into a prison escort van, a 'meat wagon', we were seated on narrow wooden slats right over the back axle. A sliding partition separated us from half a dozen men in the front. It was hot. There was no air-conditioning, no portable toilets, and no water bottles because the prisoners would want to get out to pee – a security risk. When we finally stopped and they opened the back doors we tipped out, nauseous from the fumes coming up from the exhaust and stiff as boards.

Body Search

Each time we are forced
to endure their searching hands
I stand in line waiting for my turn,
hold my breath waiting for it to pass.

They laugh and say, 'Oh, look!
The birds are spreading their wings out to dry!'
We force a smile, and with arms outstretched
submit… waiting for it to pass.

I take this problem to Him who suffered
with arms outstretched –
to the one who is waiting, knowing
all things shall come to pass.

Bandyup Women's Prison, 1987

We went through the reception routine: strip-search, shower, de-licing, given prison-issue clothing, a comb and toothbrush. There was no orientation; we were just let into the compound and left to it. We weren't wanted.

'Why didn't they keep you at Boulder? We don't want you here!' a female officer standing close by said as cell doors opened and heads peered out to get a look at the new girls. There was jeering and cat-calling.

'We don't want cop-lovers here, cunt!' (Nearly all sentences in prison include the 'f' or 'c' words and many include both.) 'You should be in the nut-house!' 'Get your head read, bitch,' other voices snarled and spat – Jenna had pleaded insanity – and she clung to me like a frightened child clings to her mother.

I reacted differently: defiantly. I decided then and there that I wasn't going to 'try to fit in', or 'settle down' as some officers advised me to do. Soon enough Jenna became angry too and between us we made a formidable couple. We wanted to be left alone (as much as you can be in prison), and we pretty much were. I was both admired and despised. Admired for my outward show of strength, and despised for my unpredictability, my refusal to go along with them. People came to accept us in time, though we never did adopt the crim's ethics and code of behaviour.

Helped by Nan's fiery temper and Spartan training I remained my own person through nearly twelve years of imprisonment, no mean feat. But all the while my real inner self was grieving and dying, shrinking and shrivelling, with only the seed of self preserved.

One of the most valuable lessons I learned inside came in my very first days. I'd lost my van, all my horse gear, my gardening tools. People who can't form strong ties with others tend to bond with their material possessions, to mistake what they have for who they are. I was like that before I went to prison, which is why I panicked when Peter said he would throw all my stuff out onto the street. But once I'd lost everything, including my sense of self, none of it mattered anymore. There was nothing more to lose. No one could hurt me anymore than I was hurting, and in that sense I felt free. I remember sitting in the compound thinking about it, marvelling at the senselessness of caring about material things.

There was one exception to this new Buddhist-like revelation. I was a heavy smoker. I just couldn't go without my 'rollies', my Drum cigarettes, and I had to work in order to buy tobacco. Jenna and I had been told we didn't have to work because we were remand prisoners, but we volunteered anyway. We were given the 'new girls' job' – cleaning ablutions. Well, we were so efficient we had them all finished within an hour. After lunch we were told to line up with the textiles workers.

Textiles women made stuffed toys, uniforms for staff and prisoners, and did other commercial sewing. It was a small factory. Jenna and I were given a huge bag of epaulettes and a pencil each to turn them inside out with. Around us the other prisoners were smirking. I realised that this was a despised job. After about an hour of mind- and finger-numbing tediousness I said to Jenna, 'I'm out of here... you stay if you want to.' Jenna was a tall, strong woman with a kind heart but something of a wild look about her. I stood up, she stood up. I went over to the officer, Jenna right behind me.

'We're off,' I said, staring hard at the officer.

'Don't be ridiculous. This is a prison! You just can't come and go as you like! Get back to work!'

We were standing beside a shoulder-high pile of synthetic stuffing. 'Let us out, or I'll drop a match in this lot!'

Eyes bulging, she ran for the phone, locking the door behind her. Two male officers were sent up on the run and within ten minutes we were back in the compound. The next day I was sent to see the psychologist, who, in a lengthy report, concluded that I had 'a problem with authority'. That was my introduction to prison life, and their introduction to me – a me I hadn't known before. My new aggression was later tempered with a more informed assertiveness. But until I learned that violence wasn't the way, I earned a reputation as being tough – not one to cross.

I was put to work in the kitchen, another locked area where violent offenders were often placed. It was a volatile work area. Once I was deep-frying fish for lunch, and a young smart alec started sloshing soapy water around my feet. She also took the grate off the fat-trap right where I was working. I told her it was not the time of day to scrub the floor but I was not in a position to stop her. I slipped on the wet floor, nearly broke my leg in the fat-trap, and badly burned my arm on the deep-fryer.

'You stupid bitch!' I screamed at her – Nan coming to the fore.

'Don't call me a stupid bitch, you white cunt!'

Then we were at it, flailing, scratching, punching each other hard until I broke the chain around her neck – a gold chain with a cross – looked at it in my hand, threw it back at her, and with blood pouring from my mouth told her 'Piss off!'

There is a point to be drawn from this vignette: a fight between female prisoners was rarely broken up by prison officers because of the fear of being accused of molestation if they happened to grab or even touch the wrong part of the body. But when sexual molestation or coercion did occur, and was reported – very rarely – it was covered up by the department. The offending officer usually lied his (or her) way out of it and nothing was done, or, if there was an unwanted pregnancy, the male officer was simply 'shipped out' to another prison. Of course, I'm talking about the 1980s, not today, when prisoners can complain to an Inspector of Custodial Services, an independent watchdog. The state ombudsman's office also is now better equipped to deal with prison complaints, but that still doesn't mean there is justice within the Justice Department.

During my early days at Bandyup I had auditory and visual hallucinations. I could hear Peter calling me in the compound, and at night through the radio. I saw a rubbish bin with a liner turn into a 'black ghost' from about a metre away, and I sometimes found myself talking to trees, coming out of a complete blank to hearing myself, and sometimes hearing other people laughing at me.

Was I schizophrenic? No. I think it was just a case of severe trauma and depression left untreated – apart from regular doses of the tranquilliser, Valium (known as 'the housewives' drug' by heroin addicts). A tranquilliser is not an anti-depressant, yet it was given to female prisoners at Bandyup for all complaints from depression to manic depression to schizophrenia, and everything in between. It was not used as a medication, but as a management tool by people who had no psychiatric training and very few social skills themselves. A lot of the female officers at Bandyup had 'come straight off a boat from England and into a uniform', as they themselves put it. Those who had any nursing background or could afford to get out often left the job within six months.

There were no call-bells in the cells in those days, so if anyone got sick during the night it was just too bad. One woman died as a result of an untreated asthma attack; call-bells were put into three of the sixty-odd cells after that. Two pages were written up into the Local and Standing Orders on the treatment of prisoners who suffered with asthma.

There were also pages of Orders written up about forbidden behavior. You weren't allowed to move outside your cell without shoes on. You weren't allowed to have another prisoner in your cell if the door was shut. When in another prisoner's cell, you had to sit on the edge of the bunk with both feet on the floor: ridiculous restraints. Men in prison are brutalised, women are infantilised. They are not allowed to wear make-up, perfume, dresses; they are not allowed to be anything other than totally dependant on their keepers – and most of all they are not allowed to be sexual.

'We all know women play with themselves, but we don't want them coming out of the ablutions block with love bites on their neck,' was the official line and love bites, tattooing and slashing up (cutting wrists and self mutilation) were punishable – it all came under the regulations of 'damaging prison property'. I remember one girl who spent a lot of time burning herself with cigarettes. She liked being punished.

CHAPTER *15*

The Trial – and Appeal

By August 1984 I was on my way back to Boulder prison and my trial in Kalgoorlie at the Supreme Court. Kalgoorlie's temperatures are colder than anywhere else in the west at that time of the year, and sitting in a damp cell wearing thin second-hand clothing doesn't help. I lost 12 or 13 kilograms in weight in just a few weeks, and had gone into a state of depression that even I didn't recognise. I no longer cared about anything, I couldn't be bothered eating, I didn't want to talk to anyone. I ended up emotionally and mentally 'numb', and because, I suspect, the superintendent at Boulder didn't want me necking myself in his prison I was sent back to Bandyup early. But I wasn't suicidal in the normal sense; I felt as though I was already dead.

I don't remember a lot about my trial, only disconnected images: the grey stone walls on the outside of the Kalgoorlie Supreme Court; a large courtroom with wooden banisters, steps going somewhere, the microphone. I remember the face of one juror, who was a young man with dark hair, a goatee beard I think, and cold staring eyes.

Justice Pidgeon was an elderly judge (unless it was the grey wig that made him look old). He wrote his notes very slowly, and appeared to fall asleep while evidence was being given at one stage. I remember seeing a detective hang his head when I was speaking, avoiding eye contact. Mainly I felt as though I was giving evidence about someone else, trying to be helpful with information.

I remember being sentenced to death, and asked if I had anything to say. What could I say? Nothing. Absolutely nothing. It was all too unreal.

The Question

When I was given the death sentence
the judge wanted to know if I
had anything to say

I should have tried to think
of something
maybe even looked guilty
for the sake of justifying jurors
and taxpayers' money

but my mind was not giving or receiving
it was as it had been on that day
so I stood detached
blindly staring at a wig
until it coughed into the silence
dismissing the court.

Bandyup Women's Prison, 1985

People want to know how I felt. Numb, detached. I felt nothing. I believe I am not the only person to have had that experience. Many people thought Lindy Chamberlain was guilty simply because she 'showed no emotion' at her trial.

This is a typical response, not an atypical one – although I do not fully understand why. It's like being in shock, all emotion suspended in time and space. I not only felt nothing, I felt as though I was a nothing, not really there, not really me, not anything. It's very difficult to put into words. And it is precisely because there is no common terminology that it is such a misunderstood and misrepresented phenomenon.

I have also been asked how I felt about having my death sentence commuted to a life sentence. It didn't mean anything to me at the time; I still had this vague idea my life was already over, almost as though I was already dead, a ghostly shell of a person watching the proceedings without much interest; being dismissed by the judge in the same manner I imagine he would flick a fly off his lunch.

It wasn't until I was escorted to the police van outside, until I reached the open air, until I stood on the steps of the courthouse, marvelling at the night sky and stars, wondering if I would ever see them again, that I regained some sense of self and feeling. Even then, I was still on another plane of reality.

I killed a man, yes. But I am not guilty of wilful murder: in Western Australia there must be intent to kill at the time of the offence and although the onus is on the crown to prove guilt beyond reasonable doubt, I was basically convicted of wilful murder because I couldn't prove my innocence. If I didn't know what was happening in my mind at the time of the shooting, how could anyone else – especially a jury of normal, reasonable people with no experience of my background? However, I was sentenced to death.

Crown: Woman silent on killing

KALGOORLIE: A crown prosecutor told a Supreme Court jury at Kalgoorlie yesterday that a 33-year-old woman had no explanation for shooting an off-duty police sergeant at Kalgoorlie this year.

Mr M. Murray told the jury that the only thing Dorothy Brenda Hodge said about the alleged incident was that she did not want to blacken the policeman's good name.

Dorothy Hodge, cleaner of Short Street, Boulder, has denied wilfully murdering Peter Robert Rafferty (38) on March 25.

Mr Murray said it would be alleged that she shot Rafferty four times about 3.30pm.

After being shot in the left shoulder Rafferty had run and hidden behind a door in a shed at the rear of his Short Street home.

Close range

When he failed to come out of the shed Dorothy Hodge had poked the muzzle of the rifle between the door and the door jamb and shot him at close range.

Mr Murray said it would be alleged that she then entered the shed and fired two other shots, both of which hit Rafferty.

Mr Murray said that after the shooting Dorothy Hodge got into her van and drove off.

About 6.30pm she went to the Kalgoorlie police station and told a police sergeant what she had done, he said.

Mr Murray said that the couple met when Rafferty was relieving at Leonora in December last year.

When Rafferty returned to Kalgoorlie she had followed him and the couple lived together at the Short Street house.

THE WEST AUSTRALIAN TUESDAY 14 AUGUST 1984

Back at Bandyup, after my trial, I had another go at suicide. I left a couple of letters to my family, and after lights out put a plastic bag over my head and tied it up. I had thought I would just pass out, but the plastic sucked in and clung to my face. I panicked and tore it off again. After that miserable failure, I decided I needed to talk to someone who knew what I was talking about, which the prison psychologist of the time didn't, so I applied to see the visiting psychiatrist, Dr Geoffrey Rollo. It was the smartest thing I ever did.

Death sentence for gun murder

KALGOORLIE: A woman who shot dead an off-duty police sergeant in Kalgoorlie earlier this year has been sentenced to death.

A Supreme Court jury in Kalgoorlie took 4 1/2 hours yesterday to find Dorothy Brenda Hodge (33) guilty of wilfully murdering Peter Robert Rafferty (38) on March 25.

Hodge, a cleaner of Short Street, Boulder, denied the charge.

During the two-day hearing the jury was told that Mrs Hodge shot Rafferty four times, once in the left shoulder, once in the small of the back and twice in the back of the head.

She told police she shot Rafferty after he made an insulting comment to her but had refused to tell anyone, including her lawyer what the comment was.

But after Mr Justice Pidgeon told her lawyer, Mr H. Wallwork QC, that if provocation had to be considered as a defence the jury must know what was said, Mrs Hodge put the comment in writing.

Mrs Hodge, who gave evidence for three hours, said that after an argument she had started to pack her belongings with the intention of leaving Rafferty.

The couple had lived at Leonora and had been living together at Boulder for about two months.

One load

She took one load of her equipment in her van to a friend's house and returned to Short Street to pick up the remainder.

It was while she was packing the rest of her gear into the van that Rafferty made the insulting remark.

"Everything seemed to slow down," Mrs Hodge said.

"I walked round the van, opened the door and got the rifle.

"Everything seemed to blacken. I looked to where Peter had been standing but couldn't see him.

"The next thing I saw was the bolt of the rifle and I fired a shot.

"I wasn't angry or upset, I didn't feel anything."

She saw Rafferty in a shed holding his hand to his shoulder. She went to the shed and saw him hiding behind the door.

She poked the muzzle of the rifle through a crack in the door and fired another shot into the back of his head.

She went into the shed and fired a further two shots at him.

"I knew I was shooting at him and knew that he would die but I didn't think about anything," Mrs Hodge said.

The last person to hang in WA was Eric Edgar Cooke in 1964. Since then death sentences have usually been commuted to life imprisonment.

Government legislation now before Parliament seeks to abolish hanging.

THE WEST AUSTRALIAN WEDNESDAY 15 AUGUST 1984

I didn't tell Dr Rollo I'd tried to kill myself – I was too embarrassed about not succeeding — but I told him about my prolonged depression.

'Of course you are depressed,' he said. 'This is a very depressing place!' At last! Someone who could see things clearly! At last, someone who would not insist it was just something wrong with me.

Dr Rollo was also the first person, in all that time, almost a year, who recognised my grief. People think that because I shot Peter I must have hated him. I never hated him. We just couldn't communicate effectively. I loved him, in my own, inferior way, and I grieved for him when I finally realised he really was dead. The healing process was painfully slow.

In my 1990 Appeal for Mercy to His Excellency, the Hon. Sir Francis Burt, AC, KCMG, QC, the lieutenant-governor and administrator of Western Australia, I made these points about the process:

> I have had a lot of counselling while in prison, and have done a lot of reading in order to try to understand both Peter's problems and my own. The psychologist at Bandyup, Mr Tony Jonikis, has said that he will confirm this counselling if need be.
>
> As I understand it, my high emotion and depression in the lead-up to the shooting stemmed from past hurts in my life (unresolved ones); and from my life-habits of suppressing fear and anger, of not talking to someone about my problems, and of accepting all the blame when something went wrong. I have slowly but surely changed my thinking habits and behaviour in these areas. I have worked on assertion training, stress management, and self-

management for depression. I suffered badly from depression during my first few years in prison: apart from the guilt and grief that I felt, there was the 'culture' shock of prison life, and I overworked myself to periodic points of nervous system burn-out.

I was treated with drugs for some time, but as I didn't want to become drug dependent, and as I have a strong aversion to the out-of-control feeling that drugs produce, I stopped taking them. That was when I started the self-management program for depression – with the guidance of Dr Rollo and the prison psychologists – and now, several years later, I am confident that I am in control of my emotions and behaviour.

Maybe a similar situation to the one I was in with Peter could place me in jeopardy of becoming out of control again; but I will never be in that situation again because I now have self-awareness, I now have an understanding of my tolerance levels, and I now have a greater awareness and understanding of other people's problems. I have no desire for another personal relationship when I am released; but if I should change my mind in later years, I will never allow the situation to get out of hand as it did with Peter and me.

The most important thing I have learned from all this is the enormity of taking another person's life. It is not like the movies, in which a person can die one week and reappear the next. Peter's life was a mess, but he may have eventually sought professional help and lived a further 40, happy and productive years if I had not killed him.

This knowledge is a terrible thing to live with. Whether in prison or not, the debt that I owe Peter and his children, the debt that I can never amend, will always be a punishment to me. I no longer punish myself to the point of disability, but nor will I ever forget what I did or stop doing some form of penance for it...

IX. Conclusion

I am now nearly 39 years old, and although I have served only half of the minimum sentence imposed upon me, I cannot see any benefit in serving another six years (with the resocialisation program).

I know that I will not re-offend (statistics support this); and my further imprisonment will not logically serve to deter other women who may unwittingly commit the same tragic offence in the future.

If, as the saying goes, I owe a debt to society, surely that debt could be better paid if I was allowed to actively contribute within society – which is what I want to do, and what I am now more capable of doing than I was in the past.

Therefore, I appeal for your mercy, and for your consideration of my early release.

Yours respectfully
Brenda Hodge.

My appeal was supported by nine written references from teachers, tutors and clergy.

'Brenda was very guarded in my early dealings with her which made getting to know her a slow process,' Jennifer Anne Atherton, my teacher at Bandyup wrote on 8 February 1990. But, apparently, I slowly let down my guard. '... by the end of her first year of university study she had earned the highest mark ever awarded in one subject and the deserved praise of her tutors... During this time, with growing confidence, Brenda also revealed all her good qualities. A witty sense of humour emerged as well as a genuine concern for her fellow students and patience and empathy with others... quite apart from being an extremely likeable and bright person, she is a pleasure to know. Brenda is a highly principled person who... I feel strongly will try to maximize her life, whatever the setting.'

Another teacher at the time, Margaret Steadman of the Department of Corrective Services, said, 'I have the highest regard for Brenda both as a student and as a person... She has a personal and intellectual courage and honesty.'

On the same day, 5 February 1990, Sister Marie T. O'Malley of the Sisters of the Good Shepherd, the Catholic chaplain to Bandyup Women's Prison, wrote, 'I believe, Sir, that the crime for which Brenda was convicted was an aberration from the normal tenor of her life... I often anguished inwardly with Brenda as she deliberately struggled through her confusion and anger to a greater understanding of herself, gradually coming to claim her own truth and to integrate all the facets of her person; seriously cultivating her psychological, spiritual and mental growth despite conditions at times uncongenial to such a task.

'...I have noticed Brenda consistently acting out of compassion and an undesigning sense of justice, reaching out to staff, other prisoners and the wider community...'

Father Peter Downes of Geraldton was candid. Urging my early release, he noted in passing:

'...I find it amusing that when she is critical of something her language can revert to expressions attributed to the profession of shearer's cook.'

Father Brenton Taylor, also of Geraldton, was more circumspect. 'I know Brenda to be a well-informed, well-educated, compassionate person who shows
a deep and genuine concern for those in unfortunate circumstances,' he wrote. 'Brenda has much to teach me by way of her life experience, her tolerance and understanding.'

Three friends from the Ministry of Education's Distance Education Centre supported my appeal. Maurice Jones: '...I had here a student of exceptional ability, probably among the half-dozen most gifted I had encountered in nearly thirty years of teaching matriculation-level students... she has a great deal to offer others... as a friend I am happy to be among those eager to welcome her return to the mainstream of life.'

Margaret Gordon: 'I have been in regular correspondence with Brenda and regard her as a friend... It has been exciting to see her achieve outstanding academic results... she has much to offer the community.'

And Janet Milward: 'Brenda's development during her time in prison may be seen as vindication of the rehabilitation system.'

My appeal was answered in a one-page letter from the secretary of the Parole Board. It read in part:

'The Hon. Minister has recently advised the Board that the recommendation made is approved and that your case should be listed for review in September 1994, some six months earlier than provided for by statute... Accordingly, you case will be listed for review by the Board in early September, 1994.'

I lost. I had to wait another four years for the next review.

On a life sentence in Western Australia, a review date does not mean a release date. It means the offender is reviewed by the parole board at that time, but may be rejected for a pre-release program, in which case they will have to wait another three years for the next review.

'Strict security life' means the prisoner must serve all his or her time in a maximum security prison. A 'life' sentence is still indeterminate, that is, the parole board may continue rejecting release applications forever, but the prisoner can shift through the system to lower security positions, as I did.

Western Australia now has higher review dates, and a 'never to be released' sentence for worst cases. This last sentence change was objected to by the Prison Officers Union, because a person who has no hope of release is a danger to officers, prisoners, and even themselves. However the public keeps calling for harsher sentences, and getting them.

Usually, the security ratings change on a third plus third basis: one-third maximum, one-third medium, the last third low security. On a life sentence, this is based on the minimum review date. As it was, I was dropped to medium security and transferred to Greenough Regional Prison in 1988. My Appeal for Mercy was refused in May 1990.

Dr Rollo continued to work without remuneration on my behalf, as had Henry Wallwork. Mr Henry Wallwork QC and his assistant counsel, Tom Percy, paid their way to go to Canberra and present my High Court appeal. The High Court found there were flaws in the trial and recommended I be given the least possible sentence for my crime under Western Australian law. I was given life with a ten-year review, rather than the strict security with a twenty-year review, and

Mr Wallwork and Mr Percy were compensated for the money they'd spent on the appeal.

Mr Wallwork became a judge sometime in 1990, and could no longer advise me. I said to him and to Tom Percy at the time of my High Court Appeal, 'I will never be able to repay you' but they insisted on doing it, and I'm eternally grateful to them for their sincerity and kindness. They are among several people I met on my nightmare journey who taught me real values, who impressed on me the goodness that lies within human beings.

LETTERS *to the Editor*

I was sentenced to die...

NAME & ADDRESS SUPPLIED

Sir, In response to the Catholic Weekly editorial, 'Savage Sentence', (The Record, February 8), I would like to share my own experience of being sentenced to death in the hope that your readership gain further insight from it.

I am not an Aboriginal, and my case is different to that of James Savage/Moore. However, I did kill another human being (my de facto husband), and I was sentenced to death as a result.

Although my sentence was commuted to life imprisonment, receiving the death sentence was a type of death in itself.

What I felt was total rejection - not of my act, but of my whole self. I felt that society, and all of humanity, had chopped me off from the tree of life and thrown me out with the rubbish to rot. I was allowed to live, but I became spiritually dead.

I became bitter, angry and withdrawn; I began to think that it was a sin for me to breathe and that my execution would have been preferable.

I cursed God with all the energy I could muster, then sank to the lowest depth of despair.

'So what?' some might say. 'An eye for an eye...'

Well, there are people in the world who are not so judgmental and unforgiving, people who allow the spirit of God to work through them to heal the injured soul, to raise the spiritually dead back to life.

People such as this (including some agnostics) reached out and helped me to help myself, and now I am strong to give support to other people when they are in need. Although still in prison, I am a social being once more.

The change of direction in my life can happen in anyone else's life - as long as there is a positive input from society. If society wants to be negative and vengeful, it will reap what it sows, but if society wants to reduce the violence that springs from within it, it must present an example of non-violence to its 'children' - and a major step in this direction is to abolish legalized violence.

THE GERALDTON RECORD THURSDAY 15 FEBRUARY 1990 (Letter written by Brenda Hodge)

Six years after my trial, on 23 November 1990, The West Australian newspaper reported that the High Court made a historic decision redefining the law relating to involuntary actions. 'The seven judges have broken new ground by agreeing unanimously that extreme stress can act in the same way as an external factor like a blow on the head to cause a person to act in a dissociative state.'

Dr Rollo wrote many letters on my behalf, one of which is reproduced here.

DEPARTMENT OF CORRECTIVE SERVICES • WESTERN AUSTRALIA

PRISON HEALTH SERVICE
P.O. Box 50, Fremantle. W.A. 6160.
Telephone: 432 4333   Fax: 430 6115
All communications to be addressed to "The Superintendent"

Your ref :
Our ref :
Enquiries

The Honourable J Berinson
Minister for Corrective Services
Capita Centre
14th Floor
197 St George's Terrace
PERTH WA 6000

Brenda HODGE

Dear Sir

The recent decison of the High Court regarding "Nina" as reported in the "West" of November 23 1990 (copy enclosed) is relevant to Ms B Hodge, who, in my opinion was in a state of dissociation at the time she killed Peter Rafferty.

I am aware that the Parole Board recently considered her case at your request, and made a recommendation. I enquired of the Secretary to the Parole Board if it were open to the Parole Board to reconsider her case. The Secretary advised me of his opinion that the Board is not in a position to make a further submission unless requested to do so by you.

In 1986 or 1987 I submitted a report touching on de-personalization/dissociation, in respect of Ms Hodge at the relevant time. I no longer have a copy of that report but expect it is in your file. In any case a further report could be submitted.

I feel obliged to bring this matter to your attention for consideration.

Yours faithfully

G L ROLLO
VISITING CONSULTANT PSYCHIATRIST

14 December 1990
(enc)

Although the first poem in my book, *One of Many* (Fremantle Arts Centre Press) is about being given the death sentence, very few people speak to me about that subject. It seems to be just too difficult.

A couple of kind hearts have asked, 'How does it feel... to be sentenced to death?' I answer that although the sentence was commuted, psychologically it was still a type of death to me. A letter written by me and published in the *Record* on 15 February 1990, (see page 171) gives my position on capital punishment. I wrote it anonymously because I did not want journalists seeking me out in prison. A letter presenting another point of view, one which is strong among conservative people, was published under mine.

Written by L. Banns, it is interesting to me in many respects, but in particular where it reads: 'A person convicted of wilful murder "beyond doubt" should be prepared to face execution.' The legal term is actually 'beyond reasonable doubt', and is based on the decision of ten to twelve jurors, who are deemed to be reasonable people.

But people are not infallible. Neither is the law, and it differs according to where you are tried. If a jury had heard my case in the eastern states, there is a good probability I would not have been found guilty of wilful murder because those states have a defence of 'diminished responsibility'. There was no such defence in Western Australia when I was on trial.

CHAPTER *16*

Education

There was a haven at Bandyup – the Education Centre. I stumbled on it, almost literally, the day I woke up on the cement footpath in the compound. The superintendent (The Fruit Tingle we used to call him, because of his lurid clothes) was poking his foot in my ribs.

'What's wrong with her?'

'Too much medication, I'd say,' the assistant superintendent hazarded.

I lay there, my face burning in the sun, unable to get up without falling down again. Valium did that to me – flattened me. So I was sent over to the surgery to see Sister. The Education Centre was in the same wing, and I wandered in while waiting to be taken back to the block.

Andrew Lansdowne, who was the education officer, is a well-known poet, much loved in many quarters. In time I told him I would like to be able to write 'good poetry', and he enrolled me in the Communications I course. From a book I taught myself to touch-type on an old cantankerous Remington that stretched my fingers to the limit. And as soon as I finished that course I enrolled in English and Literature courses through the Distance Education Centre (DEC). In 1985, too, I started a TAFE trade apprenticeship in cooking.

A list of my completed studies from that time, taken from a resume I wrote when I was getting close to release, amazes me when I look at it now: I was severely depressed most of the time, especially in the first years at Bandyup, and it wasn't until my last few years of study that I really began to believe I wasn't stupid.

It's easy to say I was an over-achieving adult, but there was more to it. I had a lifelong habit of covering up depression (though I didn't know the term or understand the concept when I first went to prison) and I think now I unconsciously stepped-up that habit of covering up as a means of survival. After my failed suicide attempt, I went into a frenzy of work, study, awards and accolades as a means of trying to believe I had some value, or that my life had some purpose. Whatever the case, I don't think I could do it again.

Apart from achievement having a bearing on my inner sense of self, it also affected the reactions of other prisoners and officers towards me. A lot of prisoners saw me as a threat – 'she thinks she's better than us.' Some saw me as an invaluable means of information on how to interpret the nightmarish maze of rules and regulations, codes and acts that governed our lives and kept us powerless. Some officers were genuinely pleased that I was able to 'fill in my time constructively', some were pleased because I was not a 'management problem', a few even took credit for my achievements: 'and if it wasn't for us, you'd be dead in the gutter by now.' One male officer at Greenough said to me: 'I might go and kill someone so I can get a free education in prison.' I have never had a free education. I am still paying off HECS fees now.

My academic success led to press releases claiming that women in prison could get a university degree 'if they chose to do so.' Propaganda. In my time at Bandyup only two others started a university course: a heroin addict who dropped out after her boyfriend killed himself, and another, my friend Julie, who died of an overdose. This is not to say there is a lack of input or competence from prison education officers. Most are highly motivated, dedicated, and above all patient. Jenny Atherton, an education officer I was to meet later, has been in the prison system for thirty years: she needs a medal!

My three Distance Education Centre teachers, Maurice, Margaret and Jan, were all excellent tutors and wonderful people. They sent me books, cards, letters, encouraged me, spurred me on. Maurice once drove 30 kilometres to the prison to give me his copy of Norton's *Anthology of Poetry*. I still have that book, and I treasure it. Margaret used to send me photographs of her cats and her home and her garden – reminding me there was a 'normal' world out there. And when I was getting close to release Jan offered me accommodation at her place if I was in Perth – she was dying of cancer at the time though none of us knew it. These people gave me a sense of value that my own mother and father never gave me.

Literature widened my vision, opened my eyes, mind and heart. I discovered writers and philosophers – I preferred them to be realistic rather than idealistic – Socrates, Shakespeare, Marx, Voltaire, Camus, Dostoevsky, Popper, and Foucault; writers and thinkers passionate about their work and social justice and the human condition.

I discovered spirituality within me, too. One night, crying after lock-up in my cell, I put my right hand up on the cold cement wall above my bunk. There was a palm-leaf cross on the wall, stuck on with blu-tack, and when I touched it I felt the hand of Jesus grasp mine, just as He took Peter's hand to save him from drowning on the sea of Galilee. 'Oh ye men of little faith!'

This felt like a genuine religious experience – a miracle – but I realise now it could also have been another hallucination from the dope and the medication I was on. Whatever it was, it gave me inner support, a strength to get through each day – and I will never forget it.

I was baptised in Bandyup Women's Prison on Easter Sunday, 1986, by Father Tory and another priest. Women who never usually went to Mass – bikies, junkies, fraudsters, a dozen or so, most covered in tattoos, some with nose rings or spiked 'butch' hair – were there with me, and I loved them all for coming to my baptism.

In early 1986 Andrew Landsdowne left Bandyup to work at the men's prison in Fremantle (the Limestone Lodge, as it is known colloquially). Our new education officer was Jenny Atherton, like Andrew, positive, practical, sharp and with a wonderful, natural charm. I spoke to Jenny about wanting to write to Bruce Dawe after reading this poem:

A Mother Visiting
By Bruce Dawe

Sometimes, she thinks, we have a burden laid on us
so heavy it almost seems a special honour...
Talking to her younger son in prison blue
through glass that's thicker than its millimetres,
she tells herself: So it has finally come
to this – it's like when he was little and I used to go
to see him in the hospital. What can I tell him now
to ease the mystery of his condition?
On either side, in cubicles,

the families and friends, the wives, the fiancees,
lean forward, strain to hear
the words that must suffice until next week, next month,
next year.
'Time's up!'
But not that other time which opens
with the vast prison gates to suck them in
(the loved and foolish ones, the born unlucky)
back down its corridors to echoing cells,
expelling her at the same time into a world
where her incarceration, shaped to theirs,
remains invisible to others,
waiting upon that day that seems so far
when the stopped clock will startle the whole house
by taking up its tick again, and, in life's movie,
unfreeze the frame, give motion back its meaning.

Westerley, December 1985

'Well if you want to write to Bruce Dawe write to him,' Jenny said.
So I did.

Bandyup Women's Prison
100 Middle Swan Rd
Guildford WA 6055

20th February, 1986

Mr Bruce Dawe
Darling Downs Institute of Advanced Education
Toowoomba QLD

Dear Sir

After first reading your poem 'A Mother Visiting' nearly one month ago, I wrote you a letter to say how much it touched me. I didn't send the letter, but after talking (about you) to our new Education officer today, I have decided to write again.

My father lives in Melbourne and isn't well off, but just before my trial he caught the bus over here to give me support during that time. I am 35 years old and have never even had a fine before I came to prison. It was naturally a great shock to my old dad when I was given the death sentence, and through the whole visit he cried. Through a lack of awareness I had little pain for myself, but that visit was full of anguish because he loves me so much – 'the loved one' – and because my situation was causing him distress.

'Time's up!' was torture because we knew we would not see each other again for a long time, and I knew then that my 'time' would also be his even though he still catches the bus and train to work every Monday to Friday, and mows the lawn every Sunday when it doesn't rain.

Reading your poem was like having my soul bared to the world, but it was also comforting to realise that that particular pain is understood by others.

I had to leave school when I was 14, but am catching up on my education now. Andrew Lansdown was our Education Officer during my first year here, and thanks to him, I have found an appreciation of life through Literature that I would have missed out on otherwise. I also have three wonderful correspondence tutors who go a long way past the limits of their job to help me.

I am lucky because I have gained from this experience, but I think my dad's life is like you described it – like a movie. I have sent him a copy of your poem hoping that he might also get some comfort from the knowledge that his feelings are understood by other people. Thank you for giving me the opportunity to do that.

About ninety percent of prisoners who have never written anything more than a letter home, start writing poetry after their imprisonment. Unfortunately most of it is hidden away in cupboards and is never seen. I don't know why people want to write when they get locked up, but if you do, it might be a good subject for another poem – if you don't mind me making the suggestion.

I will take the liberty of enclosing two of my own poems for your personal interest, and hope I am not being too forward by doing so. 'The Question' tries to describe my loss, and 'To Books and Their Authors' tries to describe my gain.

Thanks for your time with this letter (if the address gets it to you) and thank you for your poetry.

Sincerely
Brenda Hodge

And he replied:

Darling Downs Institute of Advanced Education

27th February, 1986

Dear Brenda

Thank you for your letter. The most pleasing thing a writer can get is a word of encouragement from someone who is living an experience he has only imagined. It is the only effective answer to those who say you couldn't possibly have any idea unless you've been through it (I've been a frequent visitor at prison farms and Boggo Road prison in Brisbane and I've always been very moved to see how families can stick together. I know how much it means to those inside, and get very angry at those silly people who think that 'prisoners are different').

Thank you also for the poems. Have you thought of publishing them? Why not try *Overland* whose address is PO Box 249, Mt Eliza Victoria 3930. I like them both – you have the art of ending well, rounding off the idea, the conversation....

Re: your comment on the number of people who want to write when they get locked up – I guess it's partly a way of touching the world beyond the wall – the way prisoners' touch hands, finger-tips with the visitors from 'out there'.

Best wishes
Bruce Dawe

Everyone in the State Tertiary Entrance Exam had to sit it at the same time and on the same day. As a maximum security prisoner, I wasn't allowed out. That was fine. Jenny set me up in the library. Outside she pasted large signs: Do not disturb, exam in progress.

The prison wing was quiet, I had the library to myself, and I had just settled in to read the questions in a delicious mix of anticipation and fear when a warder burst into the room.

'What a gorgeous day! Gorgeous!' The warder flung back the curtains, pushed open all the windows – it was blowing a gale – and went on giving me her garrulous weather report. 'On a day like this you could do anything! Just beautiful. Isn't it Brenda? Whadda you reckon?'

She wanted me to lose my temper, to tell her to f… off. Then she could charge me and send me back to the block. I sat there, fists clenched, tears in my eyes. After about fifteen minutes she left. I rolled a smoke and sat back. I had given up on the exam.

After a few puffs I calmed down. 'Stuff it! I'm a fast writer, I'll have a go!' I did as much as I could, but wasn't able to finish all the questions. When the results came through I was among the top ten in the state.

Those who have never been imprisoned, or worked in prisons, have little understanding of the reality of prison life. It is not just Prisoner mind games and power games, settled one way or the other in the next exciting episode. Every day is hell. Every day I woke up wanting to crawl away somewhere and die. If it hadn't been for the support and encouragement of my tutors, on a formal and personal basis, I would have found a way to kill myself. Studying was not just a means of filling in time and boosting my battered ego; it was a means of survival, literally.

Nearly all women think about suicide when entering prison (I can't speak for the men). Pauline Hanson – whose politics I can't abide – was not being melodramatic when she spoke of her suicidal ruminations: she was following a 'normal' pattern of despair. My friend Julie, who died of an overdose, used to joke about 'the final solution'.

'So what?' some might say. 'She killed an innocent man – let her suffer!'

Yes, I did kill an innocent man, and I am still suffering for that – release from prison isn't an end in itself. It's the beginning of another journey, one that depends on friends, that is dominated not by the love of power, but by the power of love. I count myself lucky to have so many good friends.

Prison is such a depressing place that writing about it now, going back in my mind, is depressing in itself. It was such a bitter reality, it almost leaves a sour taste in my mouth at this moment.

Every night without exception we were woken several times by a torch shone in our face. It stayed on our face until we shifted. And then, when we slept during lunch hour, we were called 'lazy'. Sleep deprivation has replaced light deprivation (dark cells) in prisons today. As usual, the authorities have gone from one extreme to the other. Julie and I used to refer to the department as 'Big Mother', an entirely apt Orwellian reference.

Prison officers get depressed also. 'I go to work, put on my raincoat, cop all the shit I have to, take off my coat and go home' I remember one of the better ones telling me. This is a type of situational depression.

My own continuing depression is both situational and biochemical. Without the proper medication, which I started taking in the mid 90s, I would go into a depressive spin for no obvious reason for up to three months at a time. I would go down into the 'black hole' and despite past experiences it always seemed as though I would never get out.

Now, after nearly ten years out of prison, I still suffer with depression, but it only lasts a few days at a time. It's not as frequent and not as debilitating. I cry a lot, but as my sister Carol said when we were getting to know each other last year: 'Thank God for Prozac!'

CHAPTER 17

Greenough on Sea

Greenough Regional Prison was known, wryly, as Greenough on Sea by the prison staff. Not far from the Indian Ocean, 400 kilometres north of Perth, it held around 150 prisoners, only about a dozen of them women.

The women were kept in one small unit comprised of two mother and baby cells, the solitary confinement cell, two single cells and two 'four outs' for tribal women who don't like being locked up alone.

For around three years, from October 1988, I was in one of the single cells, four metres by two and a half. I retreated there with my books, poems and letters. My studies became my whole life: reading, writing, typing essays, against an audio background of intermittent screaming, incessant calls over the PR, doors slamming and music wars, with disparate and loud music trying to drown out rival sounds.

Greenough was a dumping ground for Aboriginals of all tribes, mixed and left to it. When I first went there, men, women, all the different security rated prisoners except those in chokey on punishment or protection, and some officers, ate in a common, central dining room. Unlike Bandyup, we could share a table with anyone. This was good socially but not so good if someone had a point to make or an argument to settle. With the whole prison population a 'captive' audience, there would invariably be fights among the men – over a woman, or because of some tribal difference of opinion. It got so that I acquired a sixth sense. When a fight was about to erupt I went down to the tea urn near the officers' table.

Respite

In this country prison dining room
I am surrounded by men,
warriors of the West Coast,
soldiers of fortune
and would-be liberators of the oppressed.

They are eating, laughing
sharing the camaraderie of their sex,
sharing memories of what they did
and brave tales of what they are going to do
when they get out.

These are the people who break and enter
little girls, as well as shops and homes.
They have their sights set on society.
They welcome new arrivals like members
of the RSL, not showing or caring
that they are prisoners of war.

Greenough Regional Prison, 17 August 1990

Governments and government workers in general think that all Aboriginal people think the same, feel the same, and speak the same language. My friend in Bandyup – Jenna – was told to go to a meeting for Noongars. She stood up to her full height and said very loudly: 'Don't call me a dirty, stinking Noongar; I'm a Wongi!' Noongars are from the south, and Wongis are from the Central Desert. The Aboriginals around Geraldton (central west) are Yamatjis, and there's another tribe up in the Kimberleys. They all have different 'skin' (skin type) which they recognise, and they are very clannish.

Saturday Sport

It's not cricket
when you hit your opponent with the bat.

Stumps raised like spears,
poised, pointed
at members of different tribes,
black against black,
North against South or Central West

I tell you,
it's just not cricket.

Greenough Regional prison, 1994

After I graduated in 1992, I changed to full-time work in the gardens, and part-time study. Curtin University very kindly offered to let me do a Post Graduate Creative Writing course by correspondence, even though it was normally not a correspondence course. I wrote most of my poetry during this period.

Diane Beckingham, a Perth poet and illustrator, also helped me out a lot with letters, photos and copies of local writings. She was one of the producers of Private Entrance, in which two of my pieces were published. It was a wonderful encouragement for me, to see my work in an anthology and Sister Marie and my Perth tutors (at Bandyup) all went along to the book launch.

During all this study and work, there were the usual prison dramas: suicides, illegal brews, drug standovers, women having babies, ramps (cell searches), and lock-downs, the ever-offensive strip searches and the continual re-adjustment of the pecking order when new prisoners came in.

In 1987 Father Peter Downes asked Jack Ryan, a lay missionary with the Pallotines to minister to the men and women at Greenough Regional Prison. (Pallotines minister to all aboriginal people around the world, not just Australian Aborigines.) Jack and his wife Marnie had spent four years working out at Tardun – a school for Aboriginal kids out near Mullewa – and it was felt he would have a better rapport with the prisoners. He did, of course. A lot of the men called him 'Father Jack'. He attended Mass with the priest, and made a mid-week visit during which he had access to the whole prison on an informal basis. We all loved him dearly. Jack did this work – through thick and thin – for seventeen years. He died just as I was finishing this book. No one has taken his place; I doubt anyone could. When I asked Jack to write something down on his ideas about the prison system for this book, he was his usual selfless self:

When Brenda first mentioned her book and how keen she was to sit and write, I was overjoyed. Any person who has walked her road through life to be a survivor must be alive with courage, determination, tenacity, plus a deep communion with God as she sees God.

Her story is best left for her to tell in her way. Brenda always inspired me to hand in and give of my best, as I felt her quiet but sometimes stormy approach pushing me onwards. A simply wonderful life full of ups and downs and a deep generosity, particularly towards those with whom she lived in close proximity for many years, in prison. She helped many other inmates, particularly those whose education was very limited, whose literacy and understanding of the system was non existent.

Father Brenton Taylor used to pinch roses from the cathedral gardens and bring them into Mass. Their perfume had a heady effect on all of us. They were not confiscated, as the ones Sister Marie brought to my baptism were, so I divided them out and we all kept one each in our cell. When I went out to work in the gardens, I planted two rows of roses from the gatehouse to the main entrance of the prison. Most of them are still there.

He Brings Us Roses

Our parish priest
nicks roses
brings them to mass
to lay on a makeshift altar
as we pray.
Later we laugh
at the no-picking-roses rule;
we all agree
that gifts from God
are free

Greenough Regional Prison, 15 November 1992

Over the years I had two other prison visitors, Jackie Dixon and Marlene Rouse. Both were volunteers, who gave up their time for us – to help prisoners remain in contact with the outside. At some stage, though, Marlene went into renal failure and was flown out to Perth. She died clinically four times while waiting for a transplant, but after three or four years came back to see me. Two poems in my book are dedicated to her. She had a transplant eventually, and is one of my very best friends today. Marlene did more than anyone to help me adjust to life in 'the real world' after my release. It was a long and difficult process, even though I was better prepared than most.

Imprisonment doesn't work as a deterrent because it's all punishment and no reward. Being released is no reward when you have been branded for life and have nothing or no one to get out to. I couldn't even borrow money from the banks for a cheap car to get to work in, because I'd been out of the 'real world' for so long I didn't have a credit rating. I remember standing in the bank and saying, 'You just don't like me because I've been in prison.' They said, 'Don't take it personally, Mrs Hodge, it's the computer that has rejected you, not us.' That made me feel a whole lot better!

My release was supposed to happen a week before it did. The parole board sat on Fridays, and after waiting for ten and a half years, I was told, 'They didn't have time to sit on you today.' I remember venting my anger and frustration – my fear? – pacing up and down the block, swearing, raving, shouting. And alongside me was an officer, Mr Budd, saying 'Calm down Brenda, it's just the system.'

'A sewerage system works better than this one!' I shouted at him – but he stayed with me till I wore myself out.

The next Friday I was released.

CHAPTER 18

Released

My diary entry reads:

> Friday, October 20, 1995 – 11.30am Mr Bond came back to
> the block to tell me I was getting out. He said it was fate…
> Mr Dibden came down and helped out with the trolley etc.
> Joan came in straight away and said she didn't want any
> stuffing around because she had to go to "Stevo's" farewell
> lunch. I was out within ½ an hour.

Joan Schleicker was from the parole board in Geraldton. She's the only parole officer I've ever met who's worth her salt. In fact, she's one of those few people we meet in bureaucracies who we can call the 'salt of the earth'.

She took me around to Elsie Johnson's boarding house, where I was to stay. Elsie used to be a prison officer, and through another officer Mike Driscoll, agreed to be my sponsor for parole. Without her, I probably wouldn't have been released. People don't realise how complicated the system is, unless they are unfortunate enough to get caught up in it.

Elsie helped me out with things I had to learn: showed me how to use an ATM and took me down to Centrelink and CES (welfare and employment agencies), and showed where other services in town were situated.

It was a big deal for me, being able to go to the beach for a swim anytime I wanted to on my own. I just loved the sound of the water and the seagulls, the salty smell of the sea, the warm sand under my feet. I kept thinking, 'This can't last.' But it did. I was on the beach nearly every day, summer and winter, for the first few years of my release, until I bought a house further away from the sea. But I can still hear waves crashing, on the back beach, especially at night.

Sister Marie drove up to see me. She stayed for a few days, and gave me a lot of support. We went to the library and I tried to get a membership card. I was told I couldn't have one because I didn't have a permanent address. I said, in my usual loud way when I was aggrieved, 'Well I'm on parole for the next twelve months – I'm not likely to be leaving town!' I still didn't get the membership card, and Sister Marie said, 'I admire your openess and honesty, Brenda, but perhaps you should be a little more circumspect until people get to know you.' How gorgeous! She also asked me what I was going to do with my freedom. I told her without hesitation, 'I'm going to do the rowing, and let God do the steering.' I still have that attitude.

The following Tuesday, Edd came up to see me. We had a good few days together, went bike riding and walking along Geraldton's glorious beaches. Every year since then, Edd has come up and stayed with me for a week or so. Although I don't like too much regularity in my life, I do like that kind. I have a strong bond with my younger brother, Eddie.

I did three months' voluntary work at Nazareth House, an aged-care facility that once was a home for the 'orphans' who were sent out from England in the 1940s. At the same time I had an application in for a job at St John of God's hospital, which was closer to where I lived. When that job came up, I still had to walk to and from work (about half an hour each way) for another three months because I was employed as a casual, and the banks wouldn't lend me any money. Eventually, one of the girls at work had a little blue Suzuki hatch for sale – $2,000. I knew it was in good order and cheap to run, so I asked Sister Marie to lend me the money: she did, without hesitation. The car was being held for me, so when the cheque arrived I took it straight down to my bank to cash. Even though it was crossed, I thought they would give me the money – but no, 'I'm very sorry Mrs Hodge, but…' As I stood in the middle of the bank crying, the glass doors suddenly opened and in stepped an angel: Marlene Rouse, my friend Marlene.

'What's up, mate?' she asked in her breezy way.

'They won't cash my cheque from Sister Marie, I'm suppose to pick the car up today…'

'Never mind, we'll just go over the road to my bank, and get the money for you…' So there I was, standing in Marine Terrace with $2,000 cash in my bag, terrified. Marlene picked up on my feelings, as she always does, and drove me down to get the car. No one had ever trusted me that much before, and I will never forget the profound effect it had on me.

That Christmas, as I was pegging out the washing at the back of the boarding house, Daniel Rouse – one of Marlene's sons – came springing down the back stairway with a large Christmas cake in hand. In blue board-shorts, bare feet, and with long blonde dreadlocks, he gave me the cake and said, 'This is from Mum, and us. Mum told me to bring it around.' What better friends would I want in life?

The C.E.O. of St John of God's hospital said he would give me a job on my credentials alone, the same as everyone else. I was glad to hear that, because I didn't want any special favours. I have been working in the kitchen there for nine years now, and although we've had our differences, it has been a good place to work overall. My friends there held two fundraisers recently to help me out with medical bills. I thank them all.

Because I was always on the move, I didn't make any lifelong friends until after I went to prison. One of these friends is Jacki Wear, who I met five years ago, just after her mother died. A lot of my spare time is spent with Jacki, going to thrift shops, driving out of town for picnics, having a quiet cuppa together while discussing new plants in the garden. Jacki has a very large family, and I am always invited to their family gatherings. Jacki and I are like sisters.

CHAPTER 19

Carole and Janette

Now I have two more sisters, Carole and Janette. A month after the astonishing revelations of our first phone conversation, Carole flew to Perth from Sydney on 7 November 2003 to meet me and Edd and to visit Carnarvon where our mother died.

I drove down from Geraldton to pick her up from the airport. It's usually a four-hour trip but it took me nearly five: my muffler fell off (and I nearly gassed myself before someone told me to wind the windows down); I took a shortcut which led to a closed bridge and had to backtrack; and I got lost in the airport complex and took time to find Carole's arrivals gate, so I was fairly uptight by the time we met.

She recognised me first, calling out 'Brenda!'

We got on well straight away. But I still had mixed feelings. I wondered what secrets Carole might have, what pain she had suffered in life, and how that might affect our relationship. She didn't look like our mother but as we walked out of the airport I noticed she had very similar traits to Nan: head held high, chin out, straight back, and a seductive swing of the hips. As we chatted and laughed, I was suddenly afraid. Not afraid of Carole so much as reliving my old fear of Nan.

When she told me Nan had died, I felt free – free from a power struggle with a woman who could only feel good about herself when she was controlling and manipulating others. The mother-daughter relationship is always difficult during certain stages of life, but my relationship with my mother was one of fear from beginning to end.

I wanted my relationship with Carole to be one of equality, of mutual respect; two adults, different in many ways but with that special tie, the sisterly bond.

After having a good look around and getting a new muffler on the car, we booked into a caravan park at Swan Valley, a famous winemaking area north-east of Perth. From there we drove up to Chidlow, in the Darling Ranges, to meet Edd and Jack. We'd arranged to go for a picnic at Lake Leschnaultia, about one and a half kilometres from Edd's place.

Lake Leschnaultia is one of my favourite places for relaxation. I used to ride my old station mare, Yo-Yo, through the heavily timbered reserve from our farm in Mt Helena to the back of the lake. It's a spring-fed lake which was made in the early days to service the railway and timber mills of the area. The scant remains of the old Chidlow siding still remain, almost directly opposite Edd's house. Ironically, it has been replaced with a bus stop.

Although it was a beautiful sunny day, I was slightly apprehensive as we drove out to meet Jack and Edd. I thought Jack might not turn up at all. For some reason which I should, but don't, understand, Jack doesn't want the people he's living with to know I am not his biological daughter. I'd told him it didn't make any difference: he had devoted the best years of his life to us kids, and that was more than my 'real' father had done. But it was not a whim on his part, as I was to discover later that day.

Another reason for my apprehension was that Carole thought they might not like her and I didn't know how they would react to this outwardly confident replica of 'the old girl' (in many ways, but not all).

I wanted them to like her because I did. And that's what happened. Carole has the ability to lead conversations, to draw reticent people out of themselves. Overall it was a fun day, one in particular that I enjoy looking back on.

While Carole and Edd were cooking the fish, I asked Jack privately about Nan's still-birth when we lived at Wonga Park. 'It was a little girl,' he said with great sadness, tears brimming in his eyes. I was taken aback. For one thing, I had never thought of 'the still-born' as a boy or a girl, as a real person. And secondly, Jack's sudden ability to open up – even for just one brief moment – was absolutely amazing. How much more suffering had he harboured all these years? We can only guess. This made me feel closer to him, enabled me to forgive him for allowing so much to happen to me in silence. That was the real reason I was angry with him during my years in prison, and up until I learned of Nan's death.

We are such complex creatures, hiding the truth even from ourselves. On reflection I have come to believe we should allow ourselves – and others – to keep some of our self-defence barriers in place. To tear them all down would be too cruel, and perhaps counter-productive. But some things need to be understood in relation to the effect they have on others.

Jack has now agreed I can put the story of his still-born daughter in my story, as it surely affected the way he saw me as his daughter.

He gave me a home and love – I can't ask for anything more.

The next day, Carole and I caught a train down to Fremantle and spent the day sight-seeing. Then it was up to Geraldton, to plan for our trip up north to Carnarvon to learn what we could of Nan's last years.

Carole wanted to do a slow trip up, then a quick trip home. It didn't make any difference to me, but she was stalling, putting off going to the Carnarvon undertakers to pick up whatever paperwork and information they had on Nan. I can see how daunting it would be, trying to 'find' your mother, yet not knowing what's around the corner.

For days we went north, a leisurely route that took us to Kalbarai, Denham, Monkey Mia (where we saw a baby dolphin), and then, finally, Carnarvon appeared on the horizon.

We booked in to a caravan park and drove into town. Shirley Slater, the manager of the Carnarvon Library, is a genteel person, not the sort I expected would have been a friend of Nan's – or Beryl, as she knew her. I had come in contact with Shirley earlier, when I learned of Nan's death. The friendship grew because Nan was keen on writing, and used the library a lot. She and Shirley would talk books each time she came in, and later, when she lived at Ingada Village, out of town on the other side of the Gascoyne River, Shirley would take her books. Ingada used to be an Aboriginal camp. Now it is called the Olive Laird Hostel, a palliative care centre used by blacks and whites alike. Nan, dying of cancer of the throat, went to Ingada after a suicide attempt with whiskey and tablets. But someone found her; she was taken to hospital and when she recovered went to Ingada to die.

Nan died on 22 August 1994. Six or seven years later the Carnarvon undertaker called Shirley Slater. He wanted to know when she was going to pick up Nan's ashes. She was shocked, she told me, because she thought Nan's body had been sent to Perth to be dealt with by her family. But none of us, except Danny, who had her cremated and signed the death certificate Phillip E. Mock, knew she had died. Danny had Nan cremated in Geraldton – the year before my release in the same area, the area where I now live – then shifted to New Zealand without bothering to tell Jack, Edd or me of her death.

When Shirley got over the shock she and her husband picked up Nan's ashes and drove the 65 kilometres north to the lighthouse at Point Quobba. Danny had left instructions for the ashes to be dispersed there: he said it was what Nan had requested.

There is nothing at Point Quobba except the lighthouse, a toilet, and a few shacks around the bend of the coastline. It is a spectacular place, even in its barrenness, and I'm sure the old girl would have been pleased to have her ashes cast to the four winds there.

Shirley gave us the name and address of another of Nan's friends, Shirley Lester. Nan, she told us, was 'mad, but fun' and had enjoyed the last half of her life. She was known as 'two-bottle Beryl', a name she gave herself, apparently. The story is that she took young men, never over 22 years of age, out to her room 'to teach them how to treat a woman properly.' She was discreet and no one minded, 'so when she ordered two bottles of beer, we all knew what was going on...'

Another close friend, Connie Rogers, has since shifted down the coast to Two Rocks. These three, Connie and the two Shirleys, were close friends of Nan for many years. The last time Shirley Slater saw her, at Ingada, Nan gave her a hug and thanked her for being her friend. None of them knew she was dying, and although she may have done it that way in an effort to avoid giving her friends sorrow and pain, in fact she hurt them more by not telling them, by not letting them share that part of her experience.

Nan had a knack of upsetting people, often without any awareness of doing so. One of the stories Shirley told us was typical of Nan's behavior in the early days. Danny had notified Nan that he was coming to Carnarvon to stay, and she didn't go to the bus stop to meet him. Shirley and Nan were home playing cards when he arrived in a taxi, and she treated him very coldly. But as soon as she heard he had a large sum of money in trust (compensation for a work accident), she 'sucked right up to him'.

The compensation money was in trust because he'd had a bad drug habit, more than likely acquired after being treated with morphine. Whatever the case, Danny had to apply to the trustee in Queensland before he could get access to the money. He got some of it to buy a house in Carnarvon around 1990 where he and Nan lived for a while. Then he got a girlfriend, and Nan became jealous. She tried to kick him out of his own house. They split up – I don't know the full story – and she tried to have him committed as insane in order to get control of his money and house. And Danny was her favourite child!

Carole and I went out to Ingada with Leo Cogdon, a taxi driver we met at the Port Hotel. He said he knew our mother well. Another friend from the caravan park, Gypsy, went with us too. Leo knew all the people out there, so we were well received. We just walked around and talked to whoever was sitting out in the sun: old Jingles, Sally and Claydon Dongara, Albie Dingo and Bessie Dingo's sister. At morning tea time we spoke to some of the staff. One lady, Judy Bartlett, said she remembered our mother used to walk around with earmuffs on, because of tinnitus, but as she became very ill she shifted over to a separate house to be on her own. She told me Beryl was looked after by a lady named Mary Bell. But in her last days, she wouldn't let anyone near her except 'old Cyril'.

Something clicked. 'What was Cyril's last name?' I asked.

'Baumgarten – Cyril Baumgarten.' I sat hanging on to my chair, pale and unable to speak. Carole came in. She knew straight away I'd had a shock.

Cyril was my next door neighbour. I can still see old Cyril chipping double-gees and Paterson's Curse with a hoe over the fence. I bought my house in March 1999 partly because I liked my neighbours, Cyril and Carol Kelly, along with their four grandchildren. On my days off, out in the garden, I often chatted with Cyril over the fence. When I told him I worked in a hospital, he said he'd worked with old people in a hospital in Carnarvon. I knew nothing about Ingada Village at the time, and presumed he meant the regional hospital.

Cyril was an Aboriginal elder who used to go bush, driving for the shire up north. He didn't like living in town, but in his early days he used to load asbestos and eighteen months after I first met him he died of mesothelioma. It is not the normal thing to mention the name of an Australian Aboriginal person who has died, but Carole his wife said she didn't mind me putting Cyril in my book.

After returning to Carnarvon from Ingada, Leo dropped us off at the caravan park to pick up my car. It was time to see Ken, the undertaker. Carole was dithering when I mentioned it: will we, won't we? I thought, bugger it, I'm not coming all this way and not see if Ken has got Danny's letters. So I drove around there and went in; Carole stayed in the car. The girl who spoke to me was very helpful and told me all she knew. She gave me Danny's letters to them (with his NZ address on them), but didn't have a letter for me. Her boss had told me when I first contacted him by phone that he thought Nan had left a letter for me. But he didn't have it, and the public trustees don't have it, so Danny must either have it, or it has been lost.

Carole eventually came in and joined us, having settled down a bit by then. It's a very emotional matter for her, as it is for Janette. To be abandoned is traumatic for anyone, no matter what reasons may be given or conjured up. I feel that I was abandoned by my biological father, even though he said he offered to marry Nan. If she refused to marry him he would have had no say legally (his name is not on my birth certificate) about my upbringing. But this rationale does not stop me from feeling that he didn't care about me, didn't want to see me when I was young. I imagine it would be much harder to be abandoned by your mother.

Carole was soon on her way back to Perth on a Greyhound bus. But just before she left we had a call from the local newspaper, the *Geraldton Guardian*. A reporter wanted to do a human interest story on sisters finding each other late in life, and on our trip to visit our mother's last resting place. They'd heard the story from a turf writer who had been holidaying in Denham when we were there.

We thought about it for a while then agreed to do the story. Since then I have met numerous people looking for siblings, parents, children from whom they were separated early in life. They are all looking for the missing puzzle piece to their identity. And a lot of them still feel they have to whisper about their 'secret', as though it is something abnormal, something to be ashamed of.

My message to all those people is, 'shout it to the world!' Be proud of the fact that you have survived and even thrived, without the benefit of a full wholesome family – despite the tragedies that life inflicts upon us.

And from that article, through Carole's efforts, I am now writing this book. It is a daunting exercise, but exciting as well. Because of this whole turn of events, I now have a much larger family than I ever thought I would.

After Carole went back to Sydney, the publishers flew us both to Melbourne to discuss the proposition of me writing my autobiography. On the third day of our stay in Melbourne Janette drove into town to pick us up and take us out to her place. The meeting was a bit surreal to me: I couldn't stop looking at Janette while she was driving, and commented on how much more she looked like Nan in profile than Carole or me. Janette says she found the meeting exciting, and Carole didn't say what she felt: a bit like Nan in that respect.

Janette and her husband Jimmy have a large family: four children – George, Naomi, Anthoula and Miriam (twins) – and seven grandchildren. 'Janette made up for the rest of us,' Carole said, 'She is Mother Earth.'

When I look at Janette's family photograph, one with seventeen people, I feel very comfortable, glad that at least one of us had a normal family life. Carole, on the other hand, can't handle the large family scene. I guess it's a matter of how she sees herself, that is, someone not part of a large family. Her adoptive parents died while she was still fairly young and she had to make her own way in life thinking she had no family.

So I can understand why she didn't want to go out to Janette's family home in Ivanhoe. But I wasn't going to travel all that way and not visit my other new sister and Jimmy. Jimmy comes from Greece, and he's lovely; quiet but friendly. We all got on well, and Naomi and Anthy, two of the girls, had put on a special spread for lunch. Then we went out back to see Jimmy's garden. Tomatoes and plums drying in a rack, grape vines, beans, fruit peas, a few chooks – hiding somewhere in the jungle of vegetables and fruit – and on the patio Janette's contribution, about eighty pots of orchids. I loved it, and I love the family. Despite her share of sorrow in life, I think Janette is very lucky.

I hadn't been in Melbourne for about forty years, and in some ways it was like stepping back into a bad dream. But I was keen to move past those old ghosts and do something positive with my life. Writing this story is a positive step for me and I'm hoping it will lead to positive steps being taken in other people's lives.

On the way out to Ivanhoe we stopped at Rushall Park in Clifton Hill where Nan was born and, not far from there, the terrace house she grew up in. Three sisters, aged 61, 59 and 53, together for the first time, driving around looking for our mother's birthplace.

Janette and I ring each other every second week, and I'm hoping to go back to Melbourne one day to meet the rest of her family. Carole and I had planned a full family reunion, but I don't think that is a realistic plan now. Edd doesn't want to leave his comfort zone, and Carole keeps changing her mind about her plans for the future. But that's all OK; things will happen when they are meant to.

Right now, I'm going back outside to sit under my peppercorn trees and read the paper, maybe do a crossword, or just doze off in the sun. Yes, the sun is still shining in Geraldton, even in the middle of winter. That's why I like living here. Close to the sea, close to friends. I think I am very lucky too.

Acknowledgements

My thanks to Fremantle Arts Centre Press for the use of poems from my book One of Many, also to Teresa and Julie from the Battye State Library in Perth, WA.

Many thanks to Paul Taylor for his invaluable help and guidance in the writing of this book.

And above all, my sincere thanks to all those who have befriended me and supported me, because without them I would not be here to tell this story. Among them are:

Sister Marie O'Malley, Bandyup chaplain.

Andrew Lansdowne, Jenny Atherton and other Bandyup education officers.

Maurice Jones, Margaret Gordon and Jan Millward (dec.), my Distance Education tutors.

Don Grant, Brian Dibble and Margaret McIntyre, plus all of my other tutors from Curtin University of Technology, WA.

Gratziella Weller and Rebecca Bailey, from the education centre at Greenough Regional Prison.

Father L. Tory, P. Downes, M. O'Brien, F. Phan, B. Taylor and J. Kearney for their spiritual guidance and practical help.

Jack Ryan and family, all very good friends through thick and thin.

Diane Beckingham and the writing group who sent me letters and read my poems.

Dr Geoffrey Rollo (dec.) and Dr Ross McKinnon, who both helped me to understand and deal with my depression.

Messrs Henry Wallwork and Tom Percy, who showed some real humanity in an otherwise inhumane judicial system.

All my friends at St John of God Hospital in Geraldton, WA.

Jacki Wear and family, who all accepted me without reservation and invite me to their family gatherings.

John Thomas (Jack) Mock, my stepfather, who has filled in some of the missing pieces from the early days.

Edward John Mock, my brother, who supports me in everything I do and who visited me regularly through all those years in prison.

Nan's friends in Carnarvon: Shirley Slater, Shirley Lester and Connie Rogers.

MY FAMILY TREE

MY MATERNAL GRANDPARENTS
Marie Josephine MacKenzie (nee Roberts), WA
Keith Finlayson MacKenzie, Vic

MY MOTHER
Beryl Nanette MacKenzie, Vic (1927-1994)

HER CHILDREN

Carole Baxter
(Geneva Nanette Caroline
Faye)
11-2-1945
Adopted –
father unknown

Janette (nee Sharp)
(Marguerite Dawn
MacKenzie)
1-1-1943
Adopted –
father unknown

Daniel Phillip White
– father unknown –
1947

Brenda
(Dorothy Brenda
Mowbray White)
22-2-1951

Eddie
(Edward John
Mock)
10-12-1953

MY FATHER
Harry Smith (not his real name,
not named on birth certificate)

Married with two children

EDDIE'S FATHER
(My Stepfather)
John Thomas Mock (Jack)

married Beryl 7-3-1953